Demetrick

Here's

To

Life...

Greg Parks

Newport, RI

July 19, 2009

"I Was Thinking..."

Vignettes
Of A Life
Well Spent
By
Gregory T. Parkos

Photo by January M. Parkos - 1994

*"Attitude Is
The Essence
Of Life"*
                -- Greg Parkos

This book is dedicated to those
who...

*"Dance like nobody's watching;
Love like you've never been hurt.
Sing like nobody's listening;
Live like it's heaven on earth."*
                -- Mark Twain

Table of Contents Book One of a Trilogy		
Day	Title	Page

"I was thinking…..Vignettes of a Life Well Spent"

A CAJUN FAN

The Cajun Cabin is a lively spot on "Bourbon Street" in New Orleans where the Cajun music goes on all night long while you dine on the famous crawfish and cochon that is a staple of the Cajun diet.

Sitting at a table near the band stage, I glanced at the bar and my eyes focused on a young girl waving her head left and right to the music of the energetic Cajun band as she sat there in a beautiful white dress outfit with a bare midriff and with her head slightly tilted to the right while she looked in my direction.

She was in her twenties and the fascination I had with the view was the manner in which she was chewing gum, blowing bubbles, smoking cigarettes, drinking beer, and kicking her head back and forth all at the same time. She was mesmerized by it!

The "it" was the ambiance, the sound, the joyfulness, the high spirits attendant to the Cajun sound. The roots of the Cajuns in French and African cultures makes it a truly unique experience and quite at home in Louisiana.

It was a delightful evening….I ate the Cajun food, I listened to the Cajun music, I watched that Cajun girl….and then I went back to my lonely room all by myself.

And yet, it was a night well spent!

"I was thinking.....Vignettes of a Life Well Spent"

A FAREWELL TO ARMS

I just gave away my father's deer hunting rifle to Ernesto Martinez and I hope that after 50 years of just gathering dust, it will be used again. That will be one way of reminding the world that he is still with us in some ways.

Dad probably last hunted with that rifle 50 years ago in 1953. When he died, Mom wanted me to have that remembrance of him. A strange choice since Dad never did take me out to go hunting or fishing with him.

Not his fault, not mine…it just turned out that way. When I was of an age to begin those sports with Dad, the War came along and we all had to hunker down to develop our business and get our family on the upward economic track. And by the time that we were established and the War had ended, I had grown out of the early hunting and fishing age and I was eager to move into my adult life.

Dad and I never had a conversation. He talked to me and I listened to him but we never explored orally any topic together. Many times I have wondered what a conversation with my Dad would have been like if we held an exchange of ideas. I was so much in his image; the potential for fireworks would have been great if we attempted that prior to our "mellow years".

I talk to Dad a lot since his death. He comforts me and gives me advice. Some days I am startled to see him in my mirror but I am never surprised. How proud I am to have turned into my Dad. Over these last 46 years without him I have met many impressive guys during this life but Dad is still the one who gave me my character….he is "My Hero".

A GLASS EYE

I did not fully comprehend but he was the biggest hero I had ever even conceived…..kind of ordinary height with really big shoulders and a swagger that cleared a path as he moved through any situation.

The war was over… it was 1945 and I was on the front doorstep of the Supreme Lunch, my Dad's restaurant in Newport, R.I., when I saw him coming toward me with that forceful gait and a big grin almost as wide as his outstretched arms that he thrust under mine as he lifted me aloft into his bosom… Uncle Dan was home.

In some ways, Uncle Dan was like a big brother to me even though I had never lived in the same house with him. It was about his relationship with my mother, his sister, which caused me sometimes to feel a kind of brotherhood with him. Those three Diomandes kids had been orphaned in 1918 when the Black Plague Influenza Epidemic killed both their mother and grandmother in one quick act of disaster.

The three of them, Mary, my mother, aged 10, Sophia, aged 5, and Danny, aged 3, lived with their father and his three brothers. Mary had to drop out of school to help take care of the household and especially her younger siblings. They lived like that for the next ten years and a bond was set that could never be broken. Danny was her younger brother but he was also the child that she cared for in her mother's place.

Uncle Dan was home from the war and he had embraced me upon his triumphant return.

3

The paratrooper boots, the medals on his chest, the decorated uniform, the hearty laughs and embraces were manna from heaven to this 15 year old boy who had spent the last 4 years watching all kinds of war movies, reading about all kinds of war heroes, seeing the servicemen arriving for training as young kids and then coming back a few years later as hardened men of action. He was my hero…we were blood relatives…and he had proven his courageousness and I was very proud.

What happened next is the substance of dreams that mold a life. Uncle Dan agreed to live in Newport with his wife, Florence, and I was to work with him at my father's restaurant. Within a few days, the uniform was gone forever and he settled into his civilian life.

Ironically enough, many years later I was to serve in the successor unit to the service group in which he was involved but at the time I did not really understand what it was they did, exactly, in the war. I was to find out slowly, in bits and pieces over the years as we worked together and almost always as humorous tidbits. He was a part of the Office of Strategic Services (OSS) which was responsible for all Intelligence services for the United States during the Second World War.

Uncle Dan had volunteered to enter the Army as soon as the Japanese bombed Pearl Harbor…as did all of the young men in our family. But first he had to court and marry his sweetheart, Florence. I can remember my Grandfather, his Dad, who lived with us being very happy about this turn of events. Uncle Dan knew what he wanted to do, when he wanted to do it, and he did it…it was that simple.

Unfortunately, it was how he had married another earlier in a story of young romance that ended with betrayal that he suffered, which was a family quiet item kept from youngsters like me. But that was then and another story.

4

I saw the couple, Uncle Dan and his new bride, Florence, for the first time when they came to our home on Thames Street just before he was to go off to war in 1943 and I was impressed by the differences. Uncle Dan was a large man in my eyes with a big chest and boisterous qualities and Florence was petite, quiet and thin. It was a perfect match in our family eyes and everyone was happy but scared because our young men were going off to fight a war and some of them would not be returning home.

Like so many others, Dan just went into the Army with no special goal or assignment except to fight the enemy and restore peace to his homeland. But there was something special happening as he was being processed and he had a couple of special interviews which he did not quite understand but he was in the Army and that was that.

As 1942 was unfolding it looked like the United States needed to develop a unique fighting force to engage in all kinds of intelligence activities against the enemies including espionage and sabotage behind the enemy line wherever they occupied hostile territory. Greece was just such a place since the Italians and the Germans occupied the country and it was strategically located in the war effort. The Allies would have loved to cause trouble for the occupying force thereby slowing down the Axis juggernaut. Damon S. Diomandes was a perfect fit. He was tough. He was smart. He was gutsy. He spoke Greek. He understood the Greek culture. He looked like a Greek. It was perfect so Uncle Dan was selected to be trained as an OSS agent to operate behind the enemy lines in Greece where he would blend in with the background.

Their training was like a James Bond movie....learning how to use all kinds of explosives and weapons, learning how to parachute from low heights, hand to hand combat, infiltration, breaking and entering, and so on...every skill that the most effective combination criminal-terrorist saboteur might need.

One assignment that Uncle Dan recounted was to break into a weapons warehouse near Washington and get out again undetected. To prove the success of his training mission, my Uncle Dan took a photograph from the desk of a supervisor within the munitions plant which he showed as proof to his superiors that his mission was successful.

The Greeks had another agenda...they had old scores to settle. The resistance was made up of several political groups, the Royalists, the Communists, the Democrats, the Militarists...who would rather fight each other than their common enemy, the occupying forces of Italy and Germany. And so, it failed. Impossible for independent American OSS agents to operate in such a politically charged environment.

And now, the question was what to do with this group of Greek-American highly trained experts in sabotage who could operate behind enemy lines leading guerrilla forces. It would be a shame to waste this talent in a combat infantry unit. Where else could they be used?

Why not Burma...why not against the Japanese...Why not? There were no Burmese Americans who could be trained for the job. Sabotage in Burma would slow down the Japanese thrust against China and India and cause them to start looking behind their backs rather than just charging forward.

Who were these Greek-American agents to lead? The Kachin tribesmen of Burma...who lived in small villages in a relatively primitive manner and were fiercely anti Japanese...was the best answer.

To avoid detection and to confuse enemy spies, the detachment of OSS agents left a West Coast port on a Liberty Boat outfitted with apparel suitable for freezing climates like Siberia and for tropical climates like Malaysia.

After a long zigzag journey across the Pacific, the band of "friendly terrorists" arrived in India...Calcutta...where the OSS units in the China-Burma-India area were headquartered. There was an interim stop in Perth, Australia, to regroup the ships so they could form a convoy to India. After Calcutta, Uncle Dan and a few very select men (a group of 3 from the original group of 13) went to the Nagaland to prepare for Jungle combat.

And then, Uncle Dan and his radio operator "jumped" into Burma without any fanfare and only a prayer that the Kachins would be near where he dropped rather than the Japanese. He was lucky; the tribesman saw him descending and swept him up quickly to hide him in their village since obviously the Japanese also would have seen his descending plunge. He had arrived...

...And so their War began.

Every day was another adventure. Uncle Dan lived in a hut in the middle of the village that was on short pillars to keep it above the ground and the front end of the hut had a platform extending out where he could speak to his Kachin tribe about their missions as they would gather to go out on their forays. His knowledge of their language grew out of necessity and aided with a great deal of hand and body language along the way. They had become a deadly force.

On one occasion, the target was a Japanese fuel depot behind barbed wire located on an open and flat plain some distance away from their village.
A dozen of the Kachin tribesmen went with Uncle Dan to blow up this fuel dump....it was a particularly difficult job to gain access...they dug their way under the barbed wire fence under the cover of darkness and were able to get close enough to the actual storage tanks to place their explosives in a vulnerable spot...the real trick was to get away, alive.

Because of the nature of the explosives, they only had minutes to get away from the tank area or they would have been the little sparks on top of the stupendous bonfire they were about to cause. They ran for the opening in the fence just in time because the Japanese guards had detected their movements and were flashing their spotlights across that open plain. They were out and running into the jungle just as the fuel depot exploded in a flash that lit up the whole dark night like a fourth of July celebration.

The Japanese guards were in pursuit…the race was on…and they were all on foot. The Kachins moved swiftly into the dense jungle and as they were darting in and out of the heavy brush maybe 500 yards or so ahead of the Japanese…the Kachin unit had to stop because their chief, my Uncle Dan, had to move his bowels. He stopped in his tracks, dropped his pants, squatted, defecated, pulled his pants back up and started running again…all in one swift motion. In recounting the story, Uncle Dan explained that he was never able to delay bowel movements.

The tribesmen adored their American Rambo leader, my Uncle Dan, and from time to time he liked to perform a ritual for their pleasure and adoration…..from the platform at the front end of his hut, he would stand erect and with one fast maneuver he would remove his false teeth and display them to the villagers….they had never seen such a miracle before that a man could remove his teeth and then replace them. He became like an Idol to them. This was his advice to me:

"Greg, if you would like
to become the King of Burma get yourself a Glass Eye
and when you stand before the people, remove the eye,
display it to the natives and then replace it in your eye socket.
They will make you their King."

It is this kind of humorous recall that distinguishes true heroes.

A NIGHT IN CONSTANTINOPLE

In the tradition of the Byzantines, the naming of children is designed to honor the memory of their ancestors. Mary Vanessa was given the names of both grandmothers, Mary for her maternal grandmother and Vanessa for her paternal grandmother. The exact Byzantine Hellenic name is "Panagiota Basiliki." A fascinating combination because the literal translation is "All Holy Mother of God and Queen."

Not much is told of the Byzantine Hellenes these days but they are the people of Mary Vanessa's ancestry. All four of her grandparents were born on the European shores of the Sea of Marmara in the neighboring villages of Kerassia and Platanos, Eastern Thrace, overlooking the Dardanelles about 50 kilometers from Constantinople, Capital of the Byzantine Empire.

From the beginning of history these villages were known for their fruit, especially cherries in Kerassia, and for the sunflowers which grew across the plains of Thrace around Platanos. The inhabitants were predominantly Christian and spoke a Hellenic language with a smattering of Turkish words generously added throughout. If you listen carefully at sunrise and put your ear near the earth, you can still hear the thundering hoof beats of Bucephales carrying Alexander the Great through these villages on his conquests and leaving the Hellenic language for these Thracians to keep.

As the winds of war started to blow in the Balkans just before the Great War, many of these Byzantine Hellenes of Eastern Thrace started to migrate to America. A devastating earthquake in 1912 further convinced them that it was time to leave for the land of freedom and opportunity…..but they never left their love of roots behind.

The night before Mary Vanessa's wedding, the Parkos family and all guests celebrated the roots of their forebears to spend "A Night in Constantinople" together.

On the occasion of the marriage of our
niece, Mary Vanessa Antonio
to Joseph Wheatley
We invite you to join the Parkos family's
" A Night in Constantinople "
A visit to the homeland of our Ancestors
in Byzantium
where we will all enjoy a night of
Festivities in Constantinople.
Friday, October 11, 2002 @ The Great Hall
Fall River, MA
Greg and Nadine Parkos

"Feast upon Byzantine foods while you listen to the music of the people of Constantinople by musicians who still practice the sounds of the Ottomans and especially the soulful echo of the Oud that will make you rise up on your feet to express yourself with dance. And finally you will relish with your eyes the scintillating gestures of an Oriental Dancer expressing the emotions of the Byzantine Hellenes, our people."

10

"I was thinking…..Vignettes of a Life Well Spent"

A TEAR IN MY EYE

Hard to believe that it is the middle of the day and I am flying over the Atlantic on my way home after a 10 day visit to London on business at the end of February 1997 and just before my 67th birthday.

I just was sitting here and thinking of my life and all the good things that have happened to me…which were certainly very many…and then I remembered my most significant failure…my cross to bear so to speak.

It was my being that created that life which is so tormented every day by the invisible cage in which she is trapped. My Jaclyn lives with the daily frustration of an unfulfilled promise because I am her father. Scientifically, there is a lot of evidence I could find that would indicate that I am not guilty but in my heart I know that it is my doing.

God has a way of balancing each person's life…he gave me many gifts and he also gave me a sense of morality that includes the complete assumption of true burdens and obligations and responsibility…so I will never be carefree at least not until I have finished my life on earth.

I do not know what awaits me and I have thought many times of taking my Jaclyn with me when I go, but I could not do that cowardly and angry thing…even though I thought of it as relieving her pain and the pain of those who would be left behind. I am now convinced that my role on earth is to prepare a place for Jaclyn after I am gone and I will be judged by how well I do that.

Many people expect good deeds and kindness toward them simply because I am the Patriarch of the family and have done well.

Some feel as though they are asking very little from me and that I owe them that. Some of those same good people do not remember my Jaclyn on the weekdays of her life. I will continue to be all the things I can be for all of them…but why have they forgotten my needs.

I don't need adoration or their solicitations. The greatest gift anyone could give me would be to be kind to my Jaclyn. Take her to the park or to a movie or for lunch or just call her up and say "hi". There are exceptions to the rule… there is her sister, January, and her mom Joan and Tim Moran, of course, and my wife Nadine who all give to Jaclyn their love and care.

There are also a lot of other folks who care a lot like her aunts and uncles and cousins from both sides and they each know who they are…but there are too many others who are too busy with their own lives to care about Jaclyn.

It is a sad journey. I will stop this ranting now… life is no merry-go-round….and pretty soon the music stops and I will have to get off.

Remember me by thinking about my Jaclyn.

AHH MANOULA MOU !

Every once in a while, not often but rather from time to time, when he was tired or just deep in thought my Dad would sit back, exhale a soft breath, and utter the words: "Ahh Manoula Mou". In English, those Greek words say "Oh my little Mommy." Today is Mother's Day (May 9, 1999), and I said those same words in a whisper to myself while sitting in Church in the spiritual presence of my Mother. I looked up at the Icon of the Virgin Mary at St Sophia and my Mother looked back at me with a sweet gentle smile. She was happy today and she wanted me to know it.

Two little boys came by me to stand in line for communion and the older boy (about 8 years old) placed his younger brother (about age 7) in front of him in kind of a protective bossy way. Obviously I smiled and glanced up at Mom and she knew that it was John and me standing in line at St Spyridon all over again and she smiled back to let me know that she understood my happy thought.

Maybe Mom was a little happier with me today because for the first time in my life, I placed a votive lamp in front of her Icon as my Mother's day gift to her. I liked the feeling. Perhaps I should do it whenever I am in her presence or maybe I should do it just to be sure that I will be in her presence. That is right...I will do it to be with her.

And the sermon went something like this...." That hand that held your face to her bosom, that hand that pampered your baby bottom, that hand that wiped away the tears of your hurts, that hand that was clasped in prayer when you needed it, that hand that applauded your achievements, that hand that held onto your arm when you escorted her, that hand that stroked your cheek with a loving touch...

...when you go home, bow down before your Mother and take that hand in yours, kiss it with reverence and tenderness, and then ask for her blessings."

"I was thinking…..Vignettes of a Life Well Spent"

ALICE

That woman was something else. The high cheek bones on a pretty face, a reflection of her mixed racial origins, and that absolutely stunning body perfectly proportioned from the top of her head to the soles of her feet. To view her was to lust!

Alice was the waitress at the Supreme Lunch in Newport who worked on the night shift until two in the morning every night. The line of suitors waiting to walk Alice home was endless and constant. Alice was not committed to any one man at any time. It was March 11, 1946 and the counterman working with Alice that night was the owner's son who was celebrating his 16th birthday.

At about halfway through the night shift when the business slowed down, the crew on duty set up a piece of cake with a candle for Greg to blow out with a wish. Glancing at Alice as he bent over to extinguish the candle it was clear to anyone watching what he was wishing for that night. Alice grabbed him by the shoulders and with a reverse dip bending him over at the waist planted the longest and deepest French kiss on her somewhat innocent target. Stunned, but pleased, Greg caught his breath, staggered a little bit, and then joined in the laughter that surrounded him.

Being a Monday, the restaurant was kind of slow that night so the crew was quite happy to see a tall, ruggedly handsome guy come in later and sit at the counter. Wearing the classiest double breasted suit that Greg had ever seen, he seemed to move in a theatrical way.

14

Alice waited on him and served him a piece of apple pie with a cup of black coffee. When she returned to the end of the counter, Greg whispered "Damn it, Alice, that guy is Rod Cameron, the cowboy movie star."

Alice climbed the stool next to Rod Cameron and began to chat with him and within a matter of minutes it was clear that he was also smitten. After about a half hour of banter, he left with a cheerful "So long, see you later" to the whole crew who were watching him in awe.

Greg accepted his defeat graciously and realized that, at least, he would always have the memory of that birthday kiss to keep forever.

Did he say "See you later?"

At two in the morning, Rod Cameron came back to the Supreme Lunch and sat at the counter while he waited for Alice to finish cleaning up the booths that were her responsibility. Rod took Alice home that Monday night and then again on Tuesday and then again on Wednesday, and Thursday, and Friday, and Saturday and then he was gone.

Never to return again..

Why was he in Newport?
Why the Supreme Lunch?
Why Alice?

Greg pondered these questions but was comforted to realize that he would always have that birthday kiss to remember.

Yes, Alice of the Supreme Lunch was quite a lady and "something else" indeed.

"I was thinking.....Vignettes of a Life Well Spent"

AMERICA! AMERICA!

The stillness of First Light at the break of dawn on Saturday, August 17, 1912 was broken by loud shouting from a small group gathered at the starboard rail peering into the new day...."There it is, there it is; America! America!" and with those words as the S.S. Macedonia approached Ellis Island in New York harbor came a jumping with joy on the deck of that rusty old passenger ship loaded with peasants from the Ottoman Empire searching for a new life in America. It was the Statue of Liberty standing so stately and so beautiful that each one of the young men from Kerassia, Turkey, were exploding with tears and laughter at the same time.

These young men had left their village within days of the horrible earthquake which had literally destroyed it and completed their sea journey in about two weeks. The ship sailed on past the statue to a landside station called "Castle Gardens" where they awaited on board the ship for the health inspections and the scrutiny of the immigration authorities. Silently they stood in line and prayed for acceptance.

Although the village of about 100 families was almost totally destroyed by the earthquake, only 8 young men from that little place were able to embark on a journey to America in search of a salvation for themselves and for their families. Except for three of them that were married having left their wives behind for economic reasons, they were very young and in their mid-teens although their documentation showed them as older so that they could travel alone.

One of the young men, Theodosios, the son of Kyriakos who was called "Psiroukis", waited nervously for the medical personnel to look him over and then he was interrogated by the immigration officials before being ushered onto the gangplank to disembark in the land that would now be his new home for the rest of his life…..and at the foot of the gangplank with arms outstretched awaited his brother Gregory, eager to take his brother to Boston along with four of the other young men from Kerassia. The other three from the village were heading for Atlanta and Richmond to join their relatives there.

When the Balkan Wars spread like wildfire affecting the people of Kerassia, Gregory returned to Turkey in 1913 to try to save his family from the destruction….and was never heard from again. Theodosios, the son of Kyriakou Psiroukis, never felt the embrace of his own immediate family again in his lifetime until his first child was born and honored with the name "Gregory' to commemorate the big brother who had brought him to America and was lost trying to save the rest of the family.

Theodosios Kyriakos Psiroukis, an immigrant, became Theodore K. Parkos, an American, and taught his children the wonderful beauty of his adopted country that they had been born into as a birthright. At his funeral, comrades from his military service on behalf of his "New Found Land" saluted and paid tribute to Teddy Parkos, an American, who served his adopted country in war and in peace, with love and devotion from the day he walked down that gangplank…"America! America!"

"I was thinking.....Vignettes of a Life Well Spent"

AN AMERICAN PRIEST!

It had been a long springtime that year of 1942 with tumultuous news from the war front and the many agonies of the beginning of manhood. I was 12 years old and my eyes were growing bigger and bigger every day as I watched the world unfold before me.

Especially, I remember the Church. Everyone seemed so old and so old world that I could not begin to fit in. The priest spoke mostly Greek and knew very little English. He was a stern man with a black beard that evoked fear in all of us as we sat in the Greek language school. The classroom was composed of kids between 10 and 15 years of age all with different levels of competence in the Greek language. The teaching of Greek was conducted by the Priest with a pointer rod in his right hand that he was quick to use if you were disorderly in the classroom. You could see that rod coming straight for your head just as soon as his eye caught you out of line.

And then, the sunshine came to that church in Newport, Rhode Island. As the summer started to warm our climate, a new priest arrived. An American. It blew our minds...imagine a priest with no beard that spoke American, a real American ...and he was a young man who wore a smile on his face that shone with love for the children.

Father Constantine Theodore came into my life in June of 1942 and he began teaching me those values that have been in my heart ever since. The first thing he did for us kids was take us to an Ice Cream Parlor near church and for an elaborate sundae.

As we sat at that counter and indulged ourselves, I stared at that man and thought of Jesus. Father Theodore reminded me of the Sunday lessons about the ministry of our Lord: "...let the little children come unto me for theirs is the Kingdom of God." And then he took us boys to Hunter Field in the Point section of Newport to teach us how to play baseball...and after that to the YMCA to learn basketball...followed by his forming a Boy Scout troop at the church.

Along with the other young people in our community, I began to grow in the Church as a disciple of Father Theodore. I was especially honored to act as the senior altar boy walking before my revered priest as he brought the Holy Host around the church and onto the altar each Sunday. As the incense burned and the smoke curled toward Heaven from the censor I was waving in Father Theodore's path, I felt closer and closer to God. He was my idol and I tried to imitate his love of our fellow man.

This American Priest using the path of God brought us into the America that we would learn to love, honor and serve with total loyalty in peace and in war. And he educated us to have faith and to love our church.

He was a true man of God but he was also a real man who loved us no matter what our shortcomings might be. Each one of us left his warm embrace more secure in our faith and more loving of our fellow man.

The only thing he ever hit us with was his Love.

Thank You, Father Theodore.

ANCESTORS

And so it came to pass about six months ago. I had lived longer than any one of my ancestors. There was no ceremony, no awards given, and nobody even knew about it until I stumbled across the fact tonight on the eve of the beginning of my 80th year.

At 78 and a half years old, my mother's sister, Aunt Sophie, held the record until now. Her life spanned from October of 1913 until March of 1992 and she was the first one of our family born in America. Aunt Sophie was like a second mother to me as she lived with us from my birth until she married when I was eleven. This photo of us together with my daughter, January, was taken in 1982 while on vacation in Tarpon Springs, Florida.

Before that, my maternal grandfather had the distinction of being the oldest of our family. Just about everyone in our home town knew him as "Papou," the Greek title for Grandfather that I called him. He also lived with our family for just about all of my youth. Born in 1881, Papou lived until 1953. He was about 72 and a half years old when he died on the front steps while entering our Newport church, St. Spyridon, one Sunday morning .

I wonder if the next record holder will recall me as fondly as I remember my predecessors. Tomorrow is my birthday, March 11, 2009, and I am sure my successor is living today so I hope they will also think about me when they pass my final age.

Ancestors of Gregory Theodore Parkos

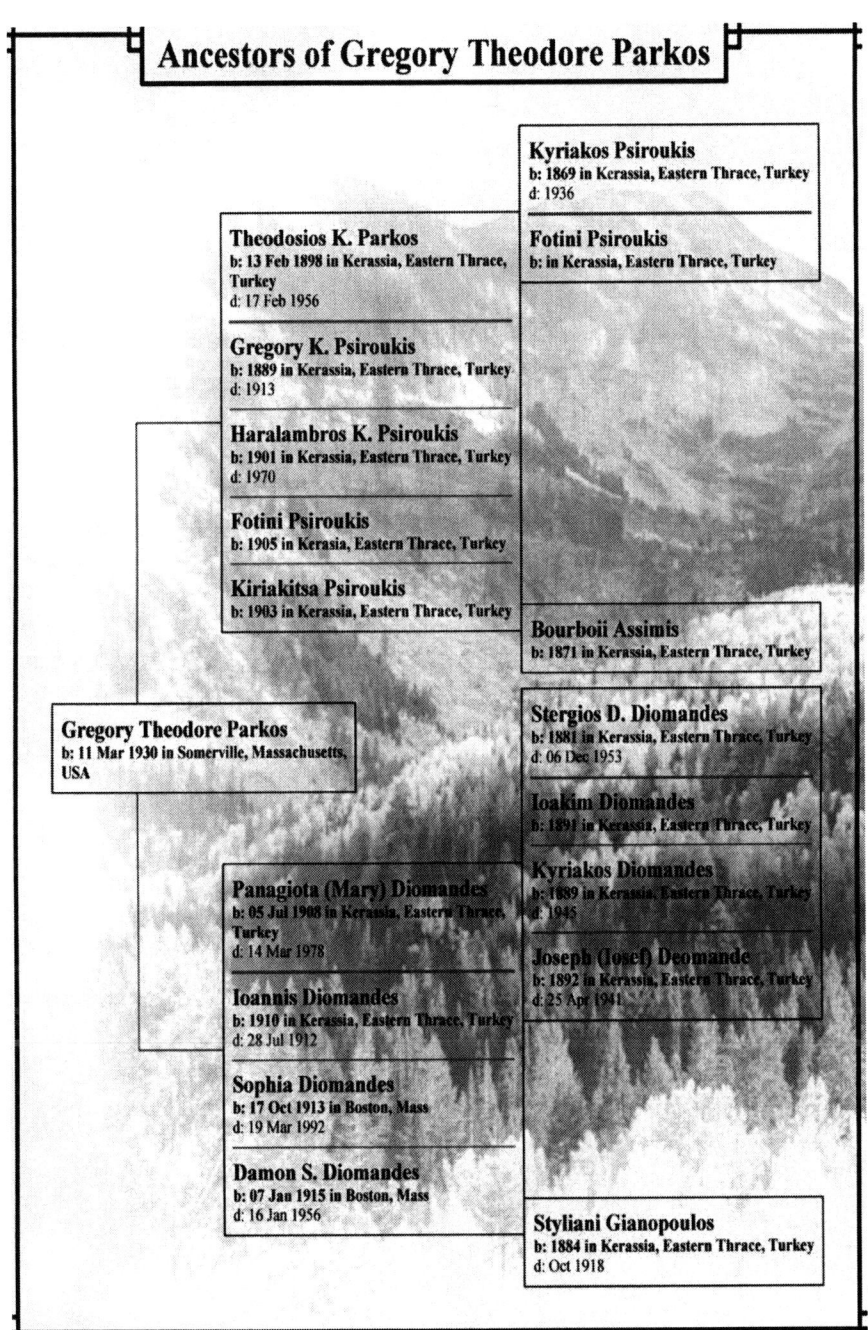

Kyriakos Psiroukis
b: 1869 in Kerassia, Eastern Thrace, Turkey
d: 1936

Theodosios K. Parkos
b: 13 Feb 1898 in Kerassia, Eastern Thrace, Turkey
d: 17 Feb 1956

Fotini Psiroukis
b: in Kerassia, Eastern Thrace, Turkey

Gregory K. Psiroukis
b: 1889 in Kerassia, Eastern Thrace, Turkey
d: 1913

Haralambros K. Psiroukis
b: 1901 in Kerassia, Eastern Thrace, Turkey
d: 1970

Fotini Psiroukis
b: 1905 in Kerasia, Eastern Thrace, Turkey

Kiriakitsa Psiroukis
b: 1903 in Kerassia, Eastern Thrace, Turkey

Bourboii Assimis
b: 1871 in Kerassia, Eastern Thrace, Turkey

Stergios D. Diomandes
b: 1881 in Kerassia, Eastern Thrace, Turkey
d: 06 Dec 1953

Gregory Theodore Parkos
b: 11 Mar 1930 in Somerville, Massachusetts, USA

Ioakim Diomandes
b: 1891 in Kerassia, Eastern Thrace, Turkey

Kyriakos Diomandes
b: 1889 in Kerassia, Eastern Thrace, Turkey
d: 1945

Panagiota (Mary) Diomandes
b: 05 Jul 1908 in Kerassia, Eastern Thrace, Turkey
d: 14 Mar 1978

Joseph (Josef) Deomande
b: 1892 in Kerassia, Eastern Thrace, Turkey
d: 25 Apr 1941

Ioannis Diomandes
b: 1910 in Kerassia, Eastern Thrace, Turkey
d: 28 Jul 1912

Sophia Diomandes
b: 17 Oct 1913 in Boston, Mass
d: 19 Mar 1992

Damon S. Diomandes
b: 07 Jan 1915 in Boston, Mass
d: 16 Jan 1956

Styliani Gianopoulos
b: 1884 in Kerassia, Eastern Thrace, Turkey
d: Oct 1918

"I was thinking…..Vignettes of a life well spent."

AND NEVER A SAINT

From the final passages of the Ancient Mariner are the haunting lines…

"Alone, alone, all, all alone,
Alone on a wide wide sea !
And never a saint took pity on
My soul in agony."
…..I really liked the absolute hopelessness of that little section.

Many ideas ago I decided to write a book about some life experiences that would be entitled "and never a saint" that would deal with some desperate times in this life.

The beginning saw our primary character ascending the staircase to the top tenement of a big city three tenement dwelling for a liaison with a married lover that would continue their mutual infidelity and his reflections on his baptism and the high hopes for that new birth. The gist of that first chapter was written and put aside and I have no idea what ever became of it.

There must be a thousand redemptions in just one ordinary life and I was certainly no exception to that. That particular falling from grace was justified in my mind by a very unfulfilled marriage and a cold bed populated by the body of a woman reeking with the smell of sweetened alcohol…a redeemed man would have ended that rotten state rather than drag himself and the lady into a tawdry affair.

It ended! And redemption began with the realization of the continuum…yes, when he realized that his child had been conceived he knew that he would never again fall from grace….now, there was a saint who cared for his "soul in agony." But that was many, many evil stories later….and we will leave those tales for another time.

"I was thinking…..Vignettes of a Life Well Spent."

AND THEN THERE WERE FOUR

The news was exciting…Camila was ours to keep ! And what a strange situation it is, Camila's biological mother had given her into adoption by a new family but the law allowed a ninety day period during which this natural mother could change her mind. On the ninety-first day the news went out to all the family that Camila was now safely a member of our family.

My mind dweledl for a long time on this child's natural mother's gift to us. Eighty-four years ago my Grandfather Stergios Diomandes arrived in America with a four year old daughter and now he is survived by 25 Great Grandchildren and 14 Great Great Grandchildren…39 so far descended from this single immigrant as I write this at the end of 1996.

The irony that has filled my heart and thoughts these last few days is that more than 10% of those two generations are within our family now because their biological mothers decided to give birth despite the fact that these 4 children were born into a non-marital status. They choose not to abort and consequently gave a gift to our family that cannot be measured in the tangible things we have here on earth. Their reward will be eternal for God must truly love them for the good they have done.

And of these natural mothers, they were all young women in their late teens and were students at the time of their pregnancy and the fourth was a simple village girl with no guile or sophistication. In each case they were the daughters in strong family environments. The details of some of them are too personal for me to share but they were each righteous and loving and that is why they gave the ultimate gift….life.
It is interesting that I do not know how many children were lost to our family because of abortion although I do know that it was at least one. Dwell on that!

23

"I was thinking…..Vignettes of a Life Well Spent."

ATHENS TONIGHT

My Collaborator/Interpreter Mario Scrivanos was driving with grim determination as we raced toward Athens in our Jeep wagon on this Friday morning. As a 65-year-old Rumanian whose private shipping vessel had been confiscated by the Communists, Mario was very passionate about our mission but not quite as passionate as his desire to return to his much younger 25-year-old Danish wife, Karen, and infant child in Athens as quickly as possible. The last ten days in Ioannina on the Albanian border had been very exhausting and not especially fruitful on this voyage. Both of us felt that we needed to regroup and start again on this mission after a long weekend back in Athens.

That morning we had a pretty big breakfast which Mario had ordered especially for us since he would be returning to the loving embrace of his bride that day…..Scrambled Eggs with Chicken Livers and a glass of sweet Greek Mavrodaphne Dessert Wine…his own personal formula especially designed to fortify an older male for his love duties to a much younger mate. Although I did not anticipate any such love duties ahead, the meal was welcomed since we would not likely be able to stop during our journey to eat another meal that day until we arrived in Athens. It took the whole day to complete our journey and we arrived at our offices at just about sunset to drop off our records and to pick up any messages we had waiting for us.

Besides the ordinary junk mail that government service imposes on its minions, there was one unusual message awaiting me which indicated that a family friend was in Athens staying with an Aunt and requesting that I call him. Nello Cotatgis identified himself as a U. S. Airman who was stationed in England and was visiting Athens.

I recognized his name as he was the son of a family that was very close to my mother. Since he was a few years younger than me, I did not really know him well but I felt that it would be fun to see him and talk about family especially since I needed to decompress a little bit. Calling him right away, I arranged for us to spend that evening together for dinner and some entertainment with one of my colleagues, Bill Crassas, who shared my apartment.

After a leisurely dinner in the Plaka at the Taberna of the Seven Brothers, we decided to take Nello to one of the Bazooki joints around town where the stars, Manolis Hiotis and Mary Linda, performed and their shows were always full of fun and the "Greek Bazooki" music was classical. They knew us well and many a night we closed the joint dancing to a sad Greek lament while smashing plates and glasses on the floor.

This particular night, something special was happening....a musical group from Turkey was being featured for a special Athens performance. Along with a great band featuring a fabulous Oud player, there were three belly dancers. The first one young nymph. She was an apprentice just learning her craft but she was lovely and innocent.

Apprentice

Another dancer was a tall, stately and beautiful former "Miss Turkey", who was also the vocalist with the group.

The third dancer was a seasoned professional who was absolutely exquisite at this dance technique and every man in the club was captured by her grace on the dance floor and many of them imagined an intimate chance encounter with her but that was not to be their luck that night.

At about 3 A.M. when the applause died down and the musicians started packing their instruments, we herded the three ladies into our vehicle, nice and snugly, and headed for our apartment for a late night session of meditation and philosophic meandering. None of the three Turkish girls spoke either English or Greek and none of us spoke Turkish. It was a beautiful party and such a compatible group to sit with and contemplate the Universe while we awaited the sunrise.

Nello paired with the young Belly Dancer as a companion.

Bill engaged the older Belly Dancer.

I communed with Miss Turkey until morning.

I have no idea what really happened that night and we only have this photo of Bill Crassas with his Belly Dancer friend at our apartment to prove there even was an "Athens Tonight."

But I sure was happy that I had eaten my breakfast that morning...........!

"I was thinking....Vignettes of a Life Well Spent"

BALLET DANCERS

My guess is that Jaclyn was about 8 years old and visiting with her Godparents in Tarpon Springs, Florida. She adored her Godparents who were my sister, Estelle, and her husband, Thomas Antonio.

Jaclyn had a lot of difficulty with speech so she choose to use an abbreviated form of the traditional salutation used by our people for the Godfather which was "Nouno" and the Godmother which was "Nouna". The nicknames she used were "No" and "Na" for them deciding to get rid of the "Nou" at the beginning of each title. No child ever had more loving and devoted Godparents than our Jaclyn.

They would do anything for her and she so loved them, and still does, that she could not even part from them when bedtime came. So, Jaclyn was attached to them day and night whenever they were together.

One night she told us that her "No" had taken her to see the Ballet Dancers and she had a wonderful time with him there.

I was shocked! Tom never displayed an interest in the Ballet as far as I knew but I knew very well that he would do anything for Jaclyn so I accepted that he even would take her to see the Ballet if she wanted to do that.

However, when I asked Jaclyn what it was like.... she let the cat out of the bag. Her story was totally honest but I had not interpreted her speech correctly....the Ballet Dancers turned out to be "The Belly Dancers" at a family restaurant in Tarpon Springs which featured Greek music, dance and cuisine.

In my mind's eye I can see "No" and Jaclyn watching the dancers every time I see the word Ballet. And that tear in my eye that washes away the scene is one of joy because Jaclyn was given the best Godparents by God to help make her path gentler and show her true love in all things...including the fine art of dancing.

"I was thinking….Vignettes of a Life Well Spent"

BARBARA'S DAY

Things were good for the Parkos family during 1939 despite the smell of war in the air. Teddy was working as night watchman for the City of Newport which gave him a steady paycheck after many difficult years. With military activity increasing in the area he took a second job as bartender at the Embassy Restaurant. The money earned was being saved to start his own business.

One particular Saturday night in March of 1939, Teddy worked as the Embassy bartender until after midnight and then he went home. He crawled into bed next to his wife, Mary, and wrapped his arms around her to warm himself. They had grown more deeply in love with each child and now that there were three of them, it was not at all unusual for them to embrace tenderly into lovemaking.

Ted was all aglow when he held Mary and whispered "do you realize that nine years ago today our Gregory was born….wouldn't it be wonderful if we just give him another sister." And then they held each other and a new child was conceived in love. Nine months later on Friday, December 8, 1939, a little girl was born to the Parkos family fulfilling the father's dream. Friday's child as related in the poem: *"Friday's child is loving and giving..."*

To name that child, Teddy dug into his deepest emotion to honor the woman whose warm arms he had left more than 27 years earlier. This beautiful brown eyed baby girl was given his mother's name, Bourboi. An enchanting rapturous blue wild flower in Turkey that gives joy to those who behold it with no need for any care. A perfect name for Teddy and his mother would live on for another generation in the soul of his daughter, Barbara. *He sobbed quietly as he held the baby - "Ah Manoula Mou"*

"I was thinking....Vignettes of a Life Well Spent"

BASEBALL STAR

In the latter part of the thirties when I was between six and nine years old living on Thames Street in Newport, the neighborhood kids spent just about every summer afternoon playing some kind of sports. Maybe a dozen pals would walk down Cozzens Court next to Integlia's Market until we faced this tall chain link fence which surrounded Cardine's Field, the local ballpark where the Sunset League played baseball.

It was generally empty when we got there so we would scale the fence to play a game of sandlot baseball with the small amount of equipment that we had lugged over the wall.

We picked sides using a technique with our only bat whereby the two captains would place their hands one over the other until one had reached the top of the bat and got the right to select the first player. Then the other Captain would select his first choice from whomever was left unselected.

I was always the last one chosen because I was the worst baseball player in the neighborhood. I couldn't play outfield because I lost sight of the ball in the air, I couldn't play infield because I would close my eyes when a grounder was heading my way, but I could bat the ball fairly well and that was that.

When we took the field I would be positioned as the catcher but not because I was good since even in that position I closed my eyes when the pitch was crossing the plate. I got to play Catcher because I was the only kid that had a Catcher's mitt, which my Dad had found in the trash at the local City Yard where he worked as the night watchman.

I guess that the moral of this story is...
"The kid with the mitt gets to catch the ball."

"I was thinking....Vignettes of a Life Well Spent"

BATTLE HYMN OF THE REPUBLIC

Awakened on the first day of March in 1998 by the sounds coming in from the Embankment on the Thames River into my hotel room at the Savoy in London...the words were familiar...."Mine eyes have seen the glory of the coming of the Lord...." and my mind went back to the same refrain being sung in the jungles of Northern Burma some 55 years ago.

Today the source of the plaintive plea is from a nationwide demonstration by the Countryside coalition, a group of rural folks protesting the attempts by Government to restrict hunting and other matters of vital interest to them. The Labour government was clearly pro Urban-Elite in their view and against the interest of the rural community. My Uncle Dan would have marched with that kind of a group because of his love of humanity and I rolled out of bed and joined the Countryside protest standing in his place.

Uncle Dan stood in his own place some 55 years ago.

Sweltering...but then, again, it always seemed to be sweltering in the jungle...just the way it is. Dan headed out of Calcutta toward the extreme Northeast of India on the Burma border for his final few weeks of training before taking his place at the head of a guerilla force of Kachin tribesmen behind the Japanese lines in the Burmese jungle.

This final training was with the Naga warriors who were to prepare Dan and his colleagues, Dean Brelis and Ernie Tsikerdanos, to survive in the jungle. These three had been selected from a very elite group of OSS Special Forces personnel to be the first guerilla leaders of that group and the whole idea was very experimental. They were the best and yet they were expendable for the "greater good".

The Naga tribe had been headhunters until their conversion to Christianity some years earlier by missionaries. As Dean Brelis told the story when I interviewed him shortly before his death:

"Danny was a hearty guy with a winning manner that displayed the embrace of friendship whenever he encountered strangers and the Naga were certainly strangers to this very small band of freedom fighters. Within an hour or two of their arrival, Danny had the Naga warriors laughing and singing and dancing in a circle. The one song that they had in common was The Battle Hymn of the Republic and they rejoiced in singing it as they frolicked at the edge of the jungle in preparation for the deadly journey into the adventure of a lifetime. Soon some of them would die and there were only two alternatives as they undertook their mission…they could win or they could lose."

It didn't take long before Danny had won them over. His happy voice resounded loudly as he wrapped his arms around the arms of these warriors in a kind of Greek line dance….and over and over again you could hear "Mine eyes have seen the glory of the coming of the Lord…He is trampling out the vintage where the grapes of wrath are stored…"

At the end of the dancing, Dan gave them his final lighthearted rejoinder: "You don't want to eat a Greek head…it is not very tasty."

Soon the training was over…and they all went off to war but that is another story.

An epitaph on the World War II Memorial in Nagaland reads:

"WHEN YOU GO HOME TELL THEM OF US AND SAY FOR YOUR TOMORROW WE GAVE OUR TODAY."

"I was thinking…..Vignettes of a Life Well Spent"

BLACK MAN

"Who do you like best: The Turks or the Greeks?" shouted the Colonel seated next to General Phil Gallagher, Commandant of the Army's Counter Intelligence Corps. This Colonel arched his straight nose and looked directly at me awaiting a reply. The third officer at the table sitting on the other side of the Commandant just looked at my dossier only glancing up at me from time to time to watch my demeanor.

Without turning away from his glare, I responded that "I am not into that Greek versus Turk thing, consequently, I would favor whatever was in the best interests of my own country." He kept challenging me brusquely saying "Your parents were born in Turkey and you speak Greek and practice the Greek Orthodox Faith, you must have some personal views or a preference."

I replied "Sorry to disappoint you, Sir, but my Dad fought in the American Army during World War I; my Uncle fought with the O.S.S. behind the Japanese lines in Burma during World War II; my brother enlisted in the Air Force at the outbreak of the Korean War; and here I sit before you in uniform awaiting orders to do what my country asks of me." Adding, "I respect my heritage but my loyalty is only to America." The Colonel continued "Would you volunteer to serve with the Greeks or Turks in Korea if assigned?" I replied "Yes, Sir."

The General spoke for the first time and said "I think we have our man here." Sixteen weeks later, finishing at the top of my class, I was appointed a Counterintelligence Special Agent, given my credentials and two separate sealed envelopes.

The first envelope contained $300 cash with instructions to purchase civilian clothes to replace my military uniforms. Obviously, my first few purchases were a trench coat, a fedora, and sunglasses for my new role.

34

The second envelope contained orders to report to 40 Broadway, New York City, where I was subsequently reassigned to the F.B.I. Boston office as the Army's representative in their Internal Security Section.

A classic Army story....threaten an assignment in combat and then send him to Wall Street instead.....every G.I. has a story like that to tell. I did get to Korea for the Sick & Disabled Prisoners of War Exchange called "Little Switch" in April of 1953 where my mission was to learn about the situation in the Chinese run Prisoner Camps especially regarding charges of brainwashing and betrayals. Also, another story for another time.

These were very exciting times during the early fifties in Boston where the Communists were using "Front Groups" to mask their activities and their agents....our task was to ferret them out. It was the time of Herb Philbrick of "I Led Three Lives" fame and many other undercover agents who later testified before Congress and became well known...and then I was whisked away...my Army term of service was over and our country had another idea for me to consider...an assignment in the Balkans.

It was now late in 1953 and just as the Comintern had set up so many fronts in the Western world earlier so did the West begin using similar fronts abroad and it had become almost impossible to decipher who was whom and what their goals were. One exception was the International Refugee Program (I.R.P.) whose goal was to aid refugees and displaced persons who were suffering as a consequence of the civil wars during the Communist insurrections in the Balkans after World War II.

In Athens, the Tameion Building, just behind the Grand Bretagne Hotel in Syntagma Square, was a multitude of various American missions operating in just about every imaginable cold war activity.

On the ground floor was the Consulate General of the United States which took care of visas for emigration once the I.R.P., which had their offices upstairs on a higher level of the building, investigated the candidates and found them to be free of any affiliation with the Communist forces that had attempted a takeover of Greece during the Civil War which ended in 1949.

Tucked into a corner of the space provided for this work were some facilities of the United States Escapee Program to which I had been assigned. The goal was to bring about the defection of important political figures from Iron Curtain Countries of the Balkans – Albania, Rumania, Hungary, Yugoslavia, and Bulgaria. The program met with great success including very high ranking Communist government officials who helped our efforts....but that is another story for another time also.

Now....skip forward some 54 years to the Terrace of the Hotel Nacional in Havana, Cuba on January 24, 2008 for a new story to be told. We were on a Church Mission to Havana in support of a Greek Orthodox Catedral built by Castro a few years ago. This evening, the ladies in our group had gone to the National Ballet of Cuba af evening of dining at the fa Hemingway bar called "El Floridita."

Six of us men de to taxi out to the Nacional home of the infamous My Lansky casino before the revolution, to enjoy a few of Cuban Rum, a few puffs of Havana cigars, and the comradeship of men telling stories to each other....some fancy and excruciatingly detailed and real...it was just great being in the company of such fine men.

As the evening turned more and more mellow, Father John Bakas started to reflect upon his youth in Greece when he and his family were displaced persons trying to migrate to America. Recalling the care packages with clothes from America and the opportunities to watch American movies and copy the acts they saw played out on the screens, Father John reenacted scenes of Cowboys and Indians and so many positive things that represented their dreams of a future in America.

The details of the stories became more and more engaging as Father John continued on to talk about his family's journey to Athens to visit the American Consulate and begin the visa procedures that were required. It was at this point that I asked him the year these events took place and he responded that it was in 1958 when he was just a young boy.

Suddenly a lot of things started falling into place as I was still serving in Greece 18 months before the events he was reflecting upon so I understood fully what he was describing. Surely, he was one of the displaced persons who were being aided by the I.R.P., all of whom were close comrades of mine. I knew exactly what he must have been going through step by step and was fascinated and paying close attention as Father John described his first encounter with a black man at the doorway to the Consulate at which point I put my glass of Rum on the table and stopped puffing on my cigar while listening in rapt attention to his story of wonder at the sight of this black man.

To Greeks from the villages, black was the color of the Devil and they were frightened seeing this Black Man at the American offices. Their first reaction was to make the sign of the cross multiple times to ward off the evil. Softly, with a cracking voice, I said "Father, I knew that man!"

"Yes, he was black but he was not from Africa" I stuttered as I tried to explain that he was Polynesian and a Maori Tribesman from New Zealand who was named "Maaka".

He was serving with the British Forces in Greece when Germany invaded in 1940. His unit was overrun before they could be evacuated to North Africa so he fled to the mountains of Crete and served with the resistance during the occupation by the Germans until the liberation of Greece in 1944

During his years in the mountains fighting as part of the resistance, Maaka marr Greek woman and had several children. He decided to remain with his family in Greece the war and worked as the doorman at the American Consulate in Athens where he was first black man that many villagers ever saw they entered these portals to a new world.

I said goodbye to Maaka in August of 1956 and Father John said hello to him in 1958....and until last month, some 50 years more or less later, neither one of us were aware that we had an acquaintance in common of importance to each of us.

Thankfor the memory, Father John.

"I was thinking…..Vignettes of a Life Well Spent"

"BLOKE" AND "YANK"

Damn, it was hot! July in Ireland does not have to be this hot but Cork is a hub city flowing with gangs of humanity sweating lots of wet humidity during these dog days. The only recourse was to indulge in a pint at the bar area of the charming combination B&B and Restaurant that was their home base for traveling in the South of Ireland.

Greg sat there with his daughter, January, 13 years old and enjoying a "roots" trip with her parents that began in Turkey, the home of her paternal grandparents, then to Thessaloniki, Greece, to visit their relatives, before  landing here in Ireland to visit the home of her Irish maternal great-grandparents.

Dublin had been fun with lots of opportunity to listen to the unique styles of Irish humor in various pubs and clubs but now they were down to the serious business of visiting January's Irish roots. It was quite natural to make Cork their home base.

They had been to Donegal and the Ring of Kerry and kissed the Blarney Stone from which area January's Maternal Grandfather's family, the McDonoughs, had migrated to the United States via the port of Cork in what were often labeled "the Coffin Ships" because so many of the immigrants died in transit due to the horrible health environment on board those vessels taking them away from the famine in Ireland.

But now, the time had come to set out for the Southwestern edge of Ireland to the place where her maternal Grandmother's folks lived. The day was sunny and the world was quiet as they drove in a westerly direction early in the day on dusty roads better suited for a horse and buggy than their rented automobile.

The trip was easy and so at mid-morning they decided to stop at a pub on the side of the road named "The Rusty Spike" for refreshments and a rest break. It was a small place that had a short bar with maybe a dozen stools and a half dozen tables with chairs at the other side of the room. There was a young woman sweeping the table area and Greg asked politely "Can we get a cup of coffee, Miss?"

She set aside her broom approached them with a big smile saying "I'm afraid not, but I can get you a nice hot pot of tea with Irish soda bread that is sure to please Americans," "sound great to me' replied Greg with laughter that suggested the he liked her cheerful ways.

As she was walking away, Greg noticed a middle aged man sitting at the last stool at a right angle so that he was watching these new arrivals and listening to them talk while sipping his "Tall One" of Guinness. As he saluted with his right hand and said "If you don't mind a local Bloke asking you, where are you off to today, Yank?"

Smiling at his happy manner, Greg replied "We're traveling to the town of Baltimore on the Southwest tip of this island."

"And why would you be going there" was his response to which Greg quickly answered "To take my daughter to visit the home country of her Grandmother's people." The banter felt good and Greg knew that this Bloke would be pleased to learn that Americans were seeking their roots in Ireland.

The man at the bar turned to his glass and took a few sips while Greg offered him a "Short One" of Irish whiskey to go with his draft as a token of their new friendship. As acceptance of the gift, the "Bloke' lifted the glass of whiskey to toast January with a twinkle in his eye as he asked "And what would be your Grandmother's family name, colleen?"

Because January was slow to respond and Greg wanted to continue this pleasant verbal engagement, he spit out "Their family name is "Ireton" and they are from Baltimore, Ireland."

The "Bloke' put the whiskey down half finished and then lifted it again to drain the remaining portion in a single gulp. As he wiped his lips with the back of his fist, he turned to face Greg directly and shouted "Ireton! Ireton! Them's Black Protestants."

Then he came over to the table, sat next to Greg and began apologetically explaining "You see, Yank, Henry Ireton was a General and the henchman son-in-law of Cromwell. He led his troops to murder the Irish Catholics in the 1600's. Some of his people settled near Baltimore but they are not Irish in our eyes and we have a very hard time forgiving what they did to our people."

Henry Ireton

The "Bloke" and "Yank" parted with kind words after sharing a round of "Tall Ones" and the Americans continued their journey to visit the land of the Iretons but they were never to forget the episode of the "Bloke and Yank" at "The Rusty Spike." And especially, Greg was stunned to learn an amazing piece of history from a guy sitting on a stool in a pub at mid-morning on the road to Baltimore.

41

BROTHER! BROTHER!

Princeton Street was in a state of exhilaration for the first time in almost a year….the depression had been hard and the men were without work most of the time. Dad and the Stratis boys had not had a house to paint in months and things were getting a little desperate. October of 1931 was probably the lowest point for them.

The rent was due, but then again it had been due for more than a year now and Cousin Nicola was a very loving man who would not press his Cousin Theodosios for money. As a matter of fact, Cousin Nicola's table fed the Parkos family most of the time "just until times get better" as he so kindly put it.

The exhilaration! It was October 5th and a child was due at any moment to the Parkos family. Theodosios and Panagiota already had a son who was about a year and a half old named Gregory, a roly-poly healthy child, and it was time to add to the family regardless of the economic circumstances….after all, things were bound to get better soon. And, anticipating a new addition to the family kind of erases all the other things on your mind no matter what is happening.

The scene was like from the Bible. Except that in this case, the manger was the front room on the first floor tenement of a 3 tenement house in the center of the universe for the immigrants from Kerassia, Turkey to America…Princeton Street, Somerville, Massachusetts. The landlord, Cousin Nicola, lived on the second floor with his family and the kitchen of his flat was the continuous social center for everything that was important in this Turkish-Greek-American community.

The scene was set…Dialecti, the midwife, was preparing the birthing bed with the help of several other married ladies who were in attendance.

The mother's sister, Sofia, was comforting young Gregory because he was fidgety since he could not be with his mother. The men were upstairs in Cousin Nicola's kitchen drinking and having fun while Cousin Nicola's wife "Pagio" prepared some foods for them to nibble on while waiting.

It happened at dusk…Panagiota sweating profusely as she pushed her entire insides to move the baby out and the midwife spreading the vaginal opening more and more with her fingers to ease the passage and the other ladies wiping the sweat from Panagiota's face and massaging her shoulders and arms….and then the grunting ended in a deep gasp and everyone was jolted by the loud piercing cry of the new born child.

Aunt Sofia had brought baby Gregory with her to the doorway just as the new baby emerged and when he heard that strong cry, Gregory twisted around in her arms and faced his new born sibling while the entire congregation in the room called out to him….
"Adelphos! Adelphos! (Brother! Brother! In Greek)"

Gregory had seen his brother at the moment of birth but did not understand the lifelong meaning of that beginning.

The men rejoiced about the good news, another son for Theodosios and the festivities continued on into the night except that the son was brought upstairs to meet his father for a very solemn and tearful meeting. The baby screamed out a greeting of recognition when he was placed in his father's arms.

The child was named, John, to honor his mother's younger brother who was killed in the 1912 earthquake which destroyed the village of Kerassia and motivated them to come to America just as Gregory had been named to honor the memory of his father's older brother who died during the Balkan Wars.

John and Gregory! Brother and Brother!

43

"I was thinking.....Vignettes of a Life Well Spent"

CHASTITY LOST

The War was over for Greg Parkos and I was heading home in November of 1953 for a few months off while I waited to take my post in Europe. Those two most recent years during the Korean War with the Army's elite Counter Intelligence Corps (CIC) were absolutely fabulous and filled with exciting events that more properly belong in another telling.

This story is too innocent to mix up with the adventures of a counter-intelligence agent...so let us begin. Certainly nobody would have believed this closely guarded secret even if I had been bold enough to share it with anyone, which I was not.

I was 23 years and 7 months old after finishing 2 years in the Army in a number of assignments, which had been preceded by 1 year of Graduate Studies in Boston, 2 years of College in Providence, and 4 years of High School in Newport. In every one of these situations, I was gregarious, socially very active, a varsity athlete, musically involved, and generally portrayed as "a ladies man" and that was true. I really did love the females about me and was keenly interested in them almost all the time...but....I feared rejection and was consequently shy about some matters....therefore as another winter began, I was still chaste. That's right, a virgin. Almost 24 years old and still no intimate affair with a woman.

That was a strange interlude in Newport. I was mustered out of the Army and been given a few months off before a special overseas assignment. Many important events happened that winter such as the 25th wedding anniversary of my parents when they took a holiday in Tarpon Springs, Florida, and I substituted for my Dad in the restaurant and my young 14 year old sister, Barbara, contracted tuberculosis and my parents had to return early from their vacation trip and my beloved Grandfather died and I may have "lost my cherry"

44

The town just felt great during my early time off and as the winter crawled into our lives, I became aware that there was a little "tart" of a redhead that worked at a restaurant named the Barbecue Pit where my Uncle Dan was a cook so I began to frequent that spot late in the evening and started at my self driven task of romancing this little spitfire. I had done it before many times in one way or another but never culminated the romancing, just stopping short of the ultimate act. At the time, I didn't know it would not be the same with "Georgette". She was short and small of size but with curves at all the strategic places that suggested erotica forever would be in your arms if you could bring her closely into your body. She was sought after by all the young and middle aged guys that went in and out of the Barbecue Pit without any known success. My work was cut out for me.

I started slowly with good manner and grace and used humor and personal concern to relax Georgette during our casual conversations, this would not be a slam-dunk event with Georgette, others had tried that and quickly failed. She rented a small apartment over my Dad's restaurant on Broadway where she lived with her 7 year old boy, Dale. It was easy to befriend them from time to time without any rush to my program as I was skilled at timing my romantic excursions.

The particular night that I had to make my move happened by accident as I had the use of a car and it was bitter cold, business was slow at the Barbecue Pit, and Uncle Dan was in great humor and we were all laughing together and I suggested to Georgette softly and privately that maybe I should come back at about midnight when she was finished with work. Her quiet was my answer and I knew we were on for that night.

It was really dark when we arrived at the apartment and Dale was sound asleep in their only bedroom. Georgette ushered out the babysitter and slipped open the door just a little bit to look at her son and I saw his peaceful, beautiful face on a pillow in the small double bed they shared.

45

Georgette and I were now alone in the living room and it was very dark and I was clammy and almost shaking with fear as I reviewed in my mind how little I knew about what and how to do what was going to happen next but I also knew that my personal honor would not allow me to turn back at this point. I had come too far.

As I undressed Georgette she displayed impatience and urged me on with her gasps and physical encircling of my body with her legs and arms as we were like half way on the sofa and half way on the floor and she wanted me and she wanted me now…no waiting , no foreplay, let's just do it. It was like a circus getting the clothes off from my lower body and attempting to mount her small form with the burning desire I had to finally have my first woman. My body wanted her so badly but my brain was intimidated by the fear of failure. In this case, the brain won out and my perfectly wonderful throbbing erection shriveled as I made some kind of an attempt to place it somewhere between her legs and just below her abdomen and I spilled out that warm ucky stuff somewhere nearby.

It was a disaster and I had no idea whether I had entered her vagina or not as I clothed myself and left quietly into that good night but I had been "with" Georgette and she had been kind and loving so that I knew my rendezvous would become part of the folklore of that winter in Newport. Only Georgette knew for sure. Within a few days I left and never heard another word about Georgette. I was just journeying through on my way to the rest of my life. Not a great performance but, at least, a kind of rough rehearsal for the next event which happened very soon in when I settled in my post abroad..

CHILD COMMITMENT

A Special Child Dedication Ceremony took place on Sunday, April 20, 1997 and the following was the message of that day:

Nisha, light this candle in honor of Kiana Lea

April, light this candle in honor of Camila MareeLyn

For each set of parents, these children represent the answer to many prayers....in each case not only the children but also the parents were especially chosen.

Friends and relatives have gathered together to bear witness to a dedication of commitment which dates back to the fourth century in a formal sense.

When Emperor Constantine sat upon his throne in Byzantium, adults in the little Byzantine village where Rebecca's predecessors lived were committing themselves as alternative guardians of their friends' children during those times of intrigue and terror.

At the same time, a similar ceremony was probably taking place among some of Ernesto and Osvaldo's predecessors in Palestine while the Jews chafed under the persecution of the oppressive Byzantine conqueror.

Even while the Huns and other "Barbarian migrations" were sweeping through Central Europe, there were people amongst Osvaldo and Ernesto's extended family performing a similar ritual. And as the Romans were abandoning Britain, the Scots, from whom Sandra is descended, were being expelled by the Saxons but not before they would pledge to each other to protect their children.

People were gathering in celebration of new life and dedication to children of their family and friends. All of these things were happening in the fourth century and to some extent these events affected each one of us gathered here today. This is not a new event for us.

These parents invite their families and friends to participate in a celebration we will call a Welcoming Ceremony. Through childhood, this is the circle of people who will be the child's world and culture. How family and friends relate to each other will determine what conclusions these children will draw about how life works. Therefore, this community is asked to make a conscious commitment to these children and their mothers and fathers.

But today, we especially wish to recognize a very specific dedication of service that will encompass a lifetime of care, guidance, and love for these children.

Osvaldo and Rebecca Lynn, you have been chosen to serve as moral and spiritual parents for Kiana Lea.

Ernesto and Sandra Lee, you have been chosen to serve as moral and spiritual parents for Camila MareeLyn.

What have you dedicated your life to do for these children ? It is not birthday presents and those sweet sounds of salutation that you find so endearing. This is a real commitment that goes beyond the candles, the brunch, the joy and kisses of this happy time.

True commitment will mean true sacrifice. In the years after the Second World War, I learned about this type of commitment first hand when I saw young Jewish children who had survived that devastating war in Greece because Non-Jewish friends of the Greek Jewish community of Salonika were entrusted with the care of Jewish children by parents who were being deported to their death in the concentration camps. These children were raised as their own by those who had dedicated themselves as you have today.

You will know if you have succeeded in about 15 years when this child will be sitting alone with you discussing her problems in life and asking for your advice and guidance. Just you and she, in that special relationship. Remembering that you have dedicated yourself to her care, guidance and love; walk with her, put your arm around her, dry her tears, support her resolve and let her know always that you are there for her.

I know this kind of love firsthand for my Godfather was such a man and whenever I would visit him, he would place a special chair at his right hand for me so that not only he and I knew about our special relationship but it was there for the whole world to see. Place a symbolic chair at your right hand whenever this child comes to visit you and she will remember you forever.

It does not escape us that another new bond is being established here...Kiana Lea and Camila MareeLyn are now bound together as spiritual sisters.

Since they are not ready yet to address each other, let's reach out to their maternal grandmothers to speak about them. Isabel and Barbara, will you take your grandchild and tell us your thoughts today? ....

Our family is a circle of strength and love.
With every birth and every union, the circle grows.
Every joy shared adds more love.
Every crisis faced together makes the circle stronger.

We are all now joined in a circle of love as one family and I will end our Ceremony with a quote from Edwin Markham, the poet:

"He drew a circle that shut me out -
Heretic, rebel, a thing to flout.
But Love and I had the wit to win:
We drew a circle that took him in!"

COME BLOW YOUR HORN

Sometime around the early forties, Uncle Dan married a lovely young lady, Florence Vouros, and shortly after that he left to fight the War in Burma as an OSS Agent behind the Japanese lines. As is the custom with our people, when Uncle Dan married Aunt Florence we became part of a larger family which now included her five siblings and their Father.

In those days, I was very mesmerized by Frank Sinatra who was a vocalist with the Harry James Band. As much as I liked the great attention Sinatra was receiving, I was much more enchanted by that fabulous trumpet player, Harry James. There was nothing I wanted more than to be like that bandleader standing on stage with a shiny trumpet in my hand and being adored by a multitude of pretty girl fans on the dance floor.

The band conductor at our High School offered to teach me how to play the trumpet but I needed to find an instrument to play which was not easy because our family did not have enough money for luxuries like that.

We lived on Thames Street in Newport in a second floor tenement. One evening, Aunt Florence and her sister, Marie, stopped by to visit my mother. There was nothing unusual about that except that Marie was carrying a container that looked like a small suitcase.

After about an hour or so, Marie turned to me and said "I hear you want to be a trumpet player, is that true?" I replied in a melancholy voice "I sure do, but I do not have a trumpet." Marie opened the small suitcase to reveal a shiny brass trumpet and said "this was my instrument when I was a musician and now I want you to have it to play." As she placed it in my hands, I heard her sweet voice say:

"Gregory, Come, Blow Your Horn!"

50

"I was thinking.....Vignettes of a Life Well Spent"

COMPANY OF MEN

Upon entering, the first thing that struck me was the "Company of Men" at the table partaking of what looked like a sumptuous meal and engaged in the most serious of discussions.

Ray Linn, my neighbor was holding court with a trio of his former Jordan High School students from Watts. Ray, a white guy in his late sixties, had been not only an important teacher but also a kind of mentor to these men, all African-Americans in their early fifties

They invited me to join this "Company of Men" and placed a dish for me in front of an empty chair.....I joined them quietly but with great interest in their conversation. The current subject as I took my place was the question posed by Ray on "Why do we need God when all the evil things taking place in the world were perpetrated under the banner of God's religions?" Slowly and persuasively in soft but firm voices each of the other men at the table presented their support for belief in God. I just sat and listened, then Ray turned to me and challenged me by another question "Greg, you're a believer, does your God talk to you?" My answer was "Yes, he is my buddy, my friend and I talk to him all the time." Clyde, the older of the three African-Americans, turned from his place at the head of the table to look at me directly and I had a sense that he was measuring the depth of my belief.

I really liked this "Company of Men" and felt a kind of comradeship with them. It was a good feeling. I wanted the conversation to go on and on. Ray then turned his Socratic technique to face the matter of how did these three men achieve success in their personal lives when so many others from Watts were dismally sad failures. Each man answered in his own way but it was clear that there was no easily identified reason....at the end of the day it was the random influences of many individual persons on their lives, and to a significant degree their teacher...Ray Linn.

With a little bit of lull in the conversation and still watching how Clyde was looking at me, I asked him what was the "cause" he was supporting with the red colored elastic band on his right wrist. He was silent for a moment and looked at me carefully, then reached down and pulled it off his wrist and handed it to me.
The rubber band broke in half when he had taken it off.

I held that broken Red Band in my hands and read the inscription which said "Marcus Lives."

Grover, who was sitting to my right, turned to me and in a soft voice said "Marcus was Clyde's son who died in an automobile accident on Thanksgiving."

I looked at Clyde and asked if I could keep the Red Band in remembrance of his son and he lowered his eyes and head in a gentle downward motion indicating that he was agreeable to that. His gift was very moving to me and when I left the group a short time later, I hugged each of the trio in appreciation of the friendship they extended to me that afternoon and early evening.

Marcus was a UCLA football star with a very promising future ahead of him whose achievements honored his parents shown below with him:

The next day was Palm Sunday and I took that red remembrance bracelet in my hand to Church where I lit a candle in memory of Marcus and prayed for him during services. Marcus was with me in spirit during that entire morning in Church.

At the end of the sermon, Father John Bakas, the Dean of my church, St. Sophia Cathedral, introduced to the Congregation a spiritual son of his whom he had Chrismated into our faith about 20 years earlier...he was an African-American professional football player named Marquez "Marcus" Pope, recently retired, distinguished for being the only football player in history to have played for all 4 of the California NFL teams.

The irony of events struck me and I could not get my mind off these unusual set of circumstances which I attributed to God. I greeted the famous football player and asked him to pray with me for the soul and salvation of Clyde's son Marcus. He responded affirmatively and....

The two of us stood there silently praying for Marcus.

CORRAGIO

Sure it is Italian but I like the sound of it......Corragio! This little 14 year old girl never heard it that way. To Barbara the words spoken were "*Be Brave*" pronounced forcefully but with a loving feeling by her physician and special Angel, Dr. Charles A. Serbst, as he discussed her illness that cold January day in 1954.

Barbara's parents, Mary and Teddy Parkos, were sitting with old family friends on the docks in Tarpon Springs, Florida, where they were celebrating their 25th wedding anniversary at the Pappas Restaurant.

Supping on the traditional Greek foods of their homeland and laughing continuously with Peter Stavros, a lifelong friend of Teddy who had been best man at their wedding, and his wife Helen. Also in the party that night were Teddy's Cousin Nicola and Pagio Stratis, in whose house they had first set up housekeeping when they married in 1929. It was an evening filled with good cheer and they had no idea of the dark and ominous news they were about to receive.

The picnic basket was filled to the brim as the whole group were getting dressed to go fishing on one of the local fishing trawlers when the telephone rang in Peter Stavros's house and a man identifying himself as Dr. Serbst asked to speak to Teddy Parkos. With some light sense of anxiety overcome by his natural bravado Teddy engaged in light banter with his dear friend to begin the conversation "Charlie, I am on way to go fishing for our lunch today.." and suddenly he stopped talking.

"Teddy, sorry to call you on your vacation but we have a situation that I need to discuss with you."

Visibly shaken, Teddy blurted out "What is it, Doctor, what is it?" Mary sensed something was very wrong when she heard her husband change his salutation from "Charlie" to "Doctor."

And slowly Teddy heard "Your daughter Barbara has a serious health condition and we need you folks to return so we can discuss her treatment." Pressing his friend, Teddy insisted on some indication of what was wrong. Slowly and haltingly he heard "It may be a case of Tuberculosis but we are not sure yet."

Within an hour Teddy and Mary were in their automobile and drove for thirty straight hours stopping only for food and fuel to arrive as quickly as possible at the Newport Hospital where Barbara had been placed in an isolation room. As they rushed into the hospital, Dr. Serbst was waiting for them outside the isolation room and helped them don the white coveralls garments and face masks that were required before entering the room. Tears streaming down his face as he walked into the room and looked at his little girl frightened in the bed, he pulled the face mask off and looking at Dr. Serbst said "I must kiss my child" and the good Doctor nodded approval. That passionate embrace linked 3 generations of the most love imaginable as Teddy's daughter, Barbara, had been named to honor his mother, Bourboi. The story of the next two years of treatment and pain and eventual success is a much bigger story than we can tell here. Stay tuned in!

Tonight, July 7, 2008, I met the Grandson of that Doctor and listened to my sister, Barbara, recount how Dr. Serbst helped her survive at the most desperate moments of her life with those powerful words "*Be Brave*...this will pass and you will be well again."

The emotion and tears were abundant and to watch Jim Roggero and Barbara Parkos embrace each other proved the presence of God to our lonely souls. Jimmy cried! Barbara cried! We celebrated the passion of one man's care and love for another who needed him...it was an epiphany. Thank God for the angel of mercy: *Dr. Charles A. Serbst*. As Jim left Barbara  in parting tonight, he glanced at her recent surgery of a new replacement knee and whispered "*Be Brave*."

CUPCAKE CAPER

After Good Friday services at the Greek Orthodox Church in Somerville, the women were dyeing the red eggs in Pagio's kitchen on Princeton Street. The calendar on the wall was marked with a heavy lined circle around April 12, 1931 which was the Eastern Orthodox Easter date that year. The house was alive with activity as they prepared for the great feast despite the sadness of the Depression that surrounded them. Just about everyone, except Nicola, the Patriarch of the clan, was unemployed. Nicola Stratis, a cooper by trade, sustained just about everyone within the extended family. Nicola and Pagio had a large family of kids including by age Helen (24), Sam (20), Connie (17), Arthur (13), Ralph (10), and the baby Florence (3).

His cousin, Theodosios Parkos, lived on the first floor of Nicola's tenement building with his wife, Panagiota, and their one year old baby, Gregory. Also living in that same tenement were Panagiota's father, Stergios Diomandes, and her sister, Sophia. She also had a brother named Danny who was still living with an aunt in Watertown where he was finishing high school. However, because of these special holidays he was visiting with his family here in Somerville. Since the tenement was pretty full, Danny spent most of the time upstairs bunking with Arthur and Ralph where he was like the leader of the pack since he was already 16 years old and they were 13 and 10.

Princeton Street was inclined upward like a small hill and at the top of the street facing it from a cross street was the imposing manufacturing structure of the Hostess Cupcake factory. Lots of people worked there baking and packing cupcakes into small bundles of 3 cupcakes to the package. At the front of the building was a small retail store that was a kind of factory retail outlet to sell their goods to the locals. On Holy Saturday, the day before Easter, Danny took Arthur and Ralph with him to that retail outlet to "case the joint" so they could figure out how to "cop" a few cupcakes for themselves.

The staff served customers from behind glass showcases totally enclosed from the front - the concept of stealing a few cupcakes was out of the question. However, Danny and Arthur did not give up easily so they conceived another plot to win their prize but they figured that Ralph was too young to be a party to the scheme.

That night while the adults were all attending midnight services at Church, Danny and Arthur crawled around the side of the Hostess Cupcake factory and broke into a glass window located just behind the retail shop and found their way to the storeroom.

Because of the major effort they had made to gain access they decided that rather than just a few cupcakes they should claim a reward of a full case. A full case of cupcakes packaged in bundles of three actually amounted to 360 cupcakes in total. They took the case back out the window they had opened and brought it to the basement of the tenement building where they opened it and each of them consumed a bundle of cupcakes right there and then. The rest of the case was left for future consumption. Arthur and Danny were back in bed by the time the adults returned from church and none were aware of the famous 1931 Cupcake Caper which was kept secret for many years.

The irony of life is that many years later in 1943, Ralph and Danny were teamed up again on an elite force of OSS Agents in World War II created to lead Kachin tribesmen behind the Japanese lines in Burma.....but that is another story.

1943   2003
Danny & Ralph   Arthur & Greg

"I was thinking…..Vignettes of a Life Well Spent"

DAY OF THE DEAD

On November 1, 2007 I was at the altar with a circle of Mexican-American Friends in remembrance of the "Dia de los Muertos." It started with a slow beat on the drum and the smell of incense and then prayers to Heaven and Earth as well as the four corners of the horizon. When the elder in the group called for the departed souls to come and join our celebration, I felt alone. They had prepared to receive their ancestors with flowers and candles. The altar contained the photographs of those who had passed on together with some of their favorite foods and drinks and tobacco for them to enjoy. I had brought nothing and was unprepared to receive my own memories!

When I returned home, I prepared myself to return to the altar the next day with gifts and remembrances for my departed parents. I found a photograph of them which I placed with the special cake that Mexicans prepare for this particular celebration. The other items would have to wait for the morning when I would take them to place upon the altar of the spiritual center.

This morning, with the enthusiastic help of Nadine, the other gifts were arranged together for me to take to the altar. A glass of "Raki" for Dad, a Koulouraki cookie for Mom, and a candle to keep vigil for them. I tucked the bag with these remembrances under my arm and walked a mile to the SPARC community building.

I approached the altars alone since the only other person in the place was a workman fixing some light fixtures. He only spoke Spanish so our conversation was quite short and I am sure he was wondering what I was planning as I emptied the bag and put the items on the altar so I could say my prayers and welcome the souls of my parents.

Standing there silently for a few minutes, I suddenly realized that the workman had left the area. It was obvious that he watched my every move and had observed the items I placed on the altar.

His quietly departing was his way of respecting the divine moment of my receiving the souls of my ancestors with my head bowed and a prayer on my lips.

I raised my eyes to view the entire altar and saw my parents there with all the other souls that loving descendants had also remembered.

Slowly
walking
away,
I turned
to my left, winked an eye, and
spoke out loud:"I'll be seeing you, Mom and Dad."

DEBTS SURVIVE DEATH

In 1956, I returned home from Europe to attend my father's funeral and to comfort my mother in this difficult moment.

There is a definite pattern to how funerals are managed in the tradition of the Greeks from Turkey and this one was handled in exactly the same manner. The wakes had been Americanized and no longer took place in the family home but rather were done in the established Funeral Parlors managed by the Undertaker.

There was a large outpouring of friends and family to honor my father at these wakes...the American Legion, the Order of Ahepa, the Masonic Lodge, the Police Department, the Fire Department, the City political leaders, the Clergy, and on and on...they were all at the wakes, maybe a thousand had come.

But there was another group. More important in our eyes. Like the cluster of followers that mourn the death of a Gypsy King, the friends and relatives of our family who had immigrated to the United States from that little village of Kerassia in European Turkey on the shores of the Sea of Marmara.

This group which numbered about a hundred came from hundreds of miles and encamped at the home of the deceased after the funeral. There is a traditional meal served to these folks to prepare them for their journey home...it consists of fish (the symbol of Christianity and salvation) and alcoholic spirits usually Raki or Brandy (a toast to the memory of the departed).

What takes place during this encampment and meal is not the mournful drone of laments and tears but rather the light and cheerful laughter of storytelling about the life of the one who had died. All of the stories are positive in presentation with great exaggeration and never an utterance of a negative thought except as in humor.

My father's feast was an outstanding one. Amongst his people, he had been a man with great flair and charisma in his life that was tremendously enhanced by his many exploits both real and imagined. A war hero, a lover, a friend, a dancer, a singer, a hunter, a patriot, a story teller, a political activist, and a damn smart and innovative businessman.

After the laughter and after the tearful farewells when most of the guests had left, one old friend of my parents from the village stayed behind and wanted a personal audience with me.

She was about my mother's age and she had given birth to her first child just about when I was born. The two women went through their pregnancy together every day as they lived practically next door to each other on Princeton Street in Somerville, Massachusetts. Her husband, now deceased, was a very close personal friend of my father…our families were almost like one in those days. Her son and I had spent most of our holidays together sleeping in the same bed and we had remained close through the years even though we had parted geographically and socially as the years went by.

Out of respect, I asked her to join me in a private bedroom so that we could talk out of earshot of the others who were still in the parlor of our home. She told me that since I was now the head of the family as I was the first born and a son, that she felt obligated to tell me that my father's family had an unpaid debt to her family from their days in the home village. She and her husband were from the same village where my parents were born. She had calculated that the debt was about the equivalent of around $200 in American money.

I was taken aback and although I could not possibly understand how she had converted the exchange, I reached into my pocket and gave her that amount of money. The debt had survived my father's death but it was not to be left unpaid even one more day as far as I was concerned even though I had no idea whether or not it was true.

The story does not end there. She also asked me to help her brother immigrate to the United States since she presumed I was an important official in the American Embassy in Athens. He lived in the north of Greece in a refugee village named Nea Kerassia (New Kerassia) where those Greeks who had been transplanted in the population exchange between Greece and Turkey in 1923 had been placed. I told her that I would look into it upon my return to Athens.

And I did. His file at the consular office was being processed but I decided to look into his background a little bit myself. My sources in the Military Intelligence and National Police network of Greece reported to me that her brother had been sympathetic to and believed to be a member of the pro-Communist movements during the civil war in Greece from 1944 to 1949. The consular office would not normally have been able to learn about this. The intelligence report was placed in his file and, obviously, his visa to come to the United States was not granted because of his association with the insurgency. Once I knew this information, I was obligated to report it.

I had paid my father's family alleged debt in cash and and I guess in some way I also paid her some interest on the debt by seeing that the record was complete in her brother's file. Rest in Peace, Dad.

"I was thinking…..Vignettes of a Life Well Spent"

DEJA VU

The following words were spoken by me at the wedding of Leah
Antonio and John Ketcham in Carmel on May 16, 1998:

In keeping with the oral tradition of our people, let me tell
you a story.

If you were to travel to St. Stephen's Church in the Temple
district of Bristol, England, you would find in a corner of that church
the effigy of Sir Robert Ketcham who was the Mayor of Bristol in the
early 1500's. The archives in Bristol clearly indicate that it was his
descendant, Edward, who was the first Ketcham to come to North
American in 1635 and brought with him a son named "John".

Exactly 902 years ago in the year 1096, a young knight from
Bristol, England, and the ancestor of Sir Robert heard the battle cry
of the first Crusade "God Wills It", and started out in the springtime
of that year heading for the Holy Land following a knight named
Walter the Penniless. It is quite possible that our young knight in the
year 1096 might have been named John Ketcham.

As this Crusade swept across Europe, through the Balkans,
onto the plains of Thrace, the fields of Sunflowers swinging in the
breeze were beautiful to behold. The Crusaders stopped to rest on the
banks of a beautiful blue marbleized sea known then as Propontis and
now called The Sea of Marmara (a Greek word for Marble) just
before their entrance into Constantinople.

It does not take a great leap of faith to imagine that these
Crusaders might have arrived at this place on just about May 16th
since they left England after the winter and it would take them about
two months to make their way across Europe.

63

On this seashore where Sir John stopped to rest is a very small village called in the language of the people of that region "the place of cherries" or Kirassia....famous for that black sweet fruit which the early Romans discovered here and then transplanted around the world.

Leah Antonio's family lived in that village for 2500 years before their arrival in America at the beginning of this century.

It is also likely that 902 years ago today, young Thracian maiden ancestors of Leah's with exotic Byzantine names like Styliani, Bourboi, Elaini, Fotini, Basiliki, Panagiota and Theodosia, wearing crude wooden crosses around their necks, fed bowls of fresh, cool black cherries to a knight named Sir John Ketcham and his fellow crusaders wearing a crimson cross on the front of their tunics.

I will not dwell on the rest of the First Crusade which victoriously took Jerusalem and Sir John returned home wearing the victor's crimson cross on the back of his tunic.

Had Sir John and maiden Leah married that day in Kirassia, it would have been at a place just like this and a ceremony very much like this also. Weddings were a festive celebration held in the open fields where the families of the bride and groom joined together to "crown" the young couple quite literally.

Since ancient times (as early as 800 BC) these crowns have been the heart of the traditional bonding together of two people and the forming of a new family. Under these same crowns Leah's parents were joined 39 years ago and we use them again today to join Leah and John as a sign of what is happening here today.

The first thing that happens in our traditional wedding is an Arravona, a Phoenician word that means "a promise made" (It is amazing how old our customs are). That is called the betrothal or the promise to marry.

Then as the next step, a service of crowning deposits you into each others hands as fulfillment of your promise to one another.

These crowns made of orange blossoms and myrtle leaves, emblematic of the sweetness and fruitfulness of marriage, are a sign of the bond between the newlyweds and of the glory and honor which covers them at this moment and throughout their marriage.

Leah and John are also here as symbols of the union of us all. Those of you who love John are loved by all of us who love Leah and I know that feeling is returned.

The ribbon that ties these two crowns together also ties us all together, forever.

...and may God Bless Us All...as one family.

"I was thinking.....Vignettes of a Life Well Spent"

DEMONS

Once each year in every Eastern Orthodox Church of the World, the gospel reading deals with Jesus casting out the demons from a man named "Legion" into the swine that were grazing nearby who then 'ran violently down the steep place into the lake and drowned. I reflect upon the demons that we may suffer. What are my demons? They are three!

First, I fear the demon named "Alzheimer's Disease." To be without recall of any relationship and to be dependent upon the care of others whose role is defined more as compensated labor than love is dehumanizing and I fear that situation most. I almost drowned as a young boy about age 4, and never learned to swim. Nadine tells a funny story about my fear of this dreaded illness. She says that if I really become afflicted with Alzheimer's, then she will take me out to sea on a rowboat and suggest that perhaps we should just jump into the water for a little swim. Having Alzheimer's, of course, I will not remember that I do not know how to swim so I will happily join her and the consequences are quite reasonable for anyone to assume. It's quite literately drowning this demon in the lake like the biblical story.

Next, I fear a "Stroke" which paralyzes me completely. To sit there mute while my family and friends try to make me comfortable as I wither away over time is a frightening anticipation for me. I cannot speak and I cannot respond. Why do I continue to breathe and why do I take up space in this world while I am simply a doll or puppet set in a corner to be glanced at from time to time and cared for with food and diapers until the dreary end. To drain the love and devotion of my circle in such a state makes me less of a person than I ever wish to be.

And lastly, my third demon is to end my life in poverty. Having been there before, I have no desire to depend on the kindness of others.

In each of the above three situations, I prefer to see the end of my mortal life rather than succumb to these horrible Demons. I pray to God that he will reward me with that alternative when my time comes.

DO THEY HAVE A MOVIE THEATRE?

Christmas in London…can you believe the majesty of it all?
The shops were glittering with decorations and lights to raise the spirits
of all the people. And it was 1997, Nisha's first time ever in the
magical city.

The people in the street were festive and even the taxi drivers
displayed unusual good humor in anticipation of an extra tip from the
Americans. The first stop was Harrod's…they claim it is the most
complete department store in the world…anything you could want is
available there…if you have the money.

On the first floor in the Food Halls, there were more than 200
different cheeses from around the world just in one of the glass fronted
refrigerated counters standing next to a coffee counter with exotic
beans from everywhere imaginable next to which was a bakery with
101 different shaped and style breads and a pastry counter with all kind
of sweet..maybe more than 100 different types alongside of which was
a delicatessen with cold meats and relishes of more different styles
than one could ever imagine and then a meat department with game
from everywhere and a seafood department with harvest from every
sea. It went on and on….every food imaginable.

And each floor above that stuffed with exotic goods from all
over the universe almost….Ladies clothing, Men's garments,
Children's attire, Household furniture, Souvenirs, Restaurants, Tea
Rooms, Pubs, Beauty Salons…more than one could imagine.

As they finished the shopping journey and in response to an
innocent question about how much she enjoyed her visit…Nisha
responded: "Do they have a Movie Theatre ? "

Nisha lives now in Los Angeles as I am sure you understand and
in her new home city, no shopping event is complete without a movie
theatre nearby…there is one at every mall…c'est tragicque.

"I was thinking…..Vignettes of a Life Well Spent"

DOUGHNUT

Across from Rogers High School was Ann's Donut Shop.

Each day after school from 1944 to 1948 I would stop in front of the store window to watch an automatic miniature mechanical machine grasping toy doughnuts and placing them in and out of a liquid bath imitating the process of the deep-fat cooking of the real things. It went on and on in a circular path and I was mesmerized.

But even more important to my young eyes and inquisitive mind was the small cardboard sign pasted on the window which read:

"As you travel on through life,
Let this Motto be your goal…
Keep your eye upon the donut,
And not upon the hole."

Not content with that bit of philosophy which stuck with me for the rest of my life, I added to my storehouse of wise gems a paradox explained to me by Uncle Dan with whom I worked during the summer in my Dad's restaurant "The Supreme Lunch."

"Have you ever noticed the unbalance of life?
When you sit with Coffee and a Donut,
And you proceed to dunk the Donut in the Coffee,
That, without exception, either
The Coffee is finished but the Donut is not,
Or the Donut is finished but the Coffee is not."

I have pondered those thoughts for many years now and have finally but reluctantly concluded that it is not wise to sit and dunk your donut in coffee while contemplating your choices of action during your lifetime.

EARTHQUAKE

In late July or early August of 1912, depending upon whether you use the Julian calendar or the Gregorian calendar, the final indignity to the Stergios Diamantis family in the village of Kerassia on the edge of the Sea of Mamara in Turkey was the Great Earthquake.

The patriarch of the family, Stergios, was in America where he was struggling to survive and make enough money to care for his family in "the Old Country" where he planned to return and live in comfort once he had made his "fortune." In America, Stergios had become "Stelios Diomandes" because the immigration officer could not understand what the new immigrant was telling him in response to an inquiry about his name. It was the custom of that village that no family surnames were used and his name consisted of his baptismal name followed by a reference to hs father's given name. If further identification was needed in a case where there might be confusion as to which particular family the individual belonged to, a reference might be to the family occupation or characteristic such as physical appearance.

The earthquake struck during the night while the family was asleep in a small stone house that they occupied with the father's mother, who was a widow and lived with her oldest son and daughter-in-law as was also the custom since she had no daughters, and the house came tumbling down upon them. The children of the family were Panagiota, who was 4 years old havng just recently celebrated her birthday, and a year-old baby son named Ioannis.

The crashing stones that thundered down upon this poor family crushed baby Ioannis to death and caused serious injury to Panagiota's head. When the family was rescued by fellow villagers, Panagiota's face was covered in blood and she was being held closely in her Grandmother's bosom while the dead baby Ioannis was under pile of rocks in another corner of what was the house. Fortunately, Panagiotas made a comple recovery from her injuries.

As quickly as he could, Stergios returned from America to collect his family together, bury his son, and take them all to the promised land where they would start life anew in Boston on Tyler Street where the new immigrants were establishing a community of Greeks from Turkey.

The earthquake was the final indignity for Stergios' family in Kerassia because as Greek Christians, they had been subjected to continuing abuse bythe Ottomans, an Islamic Empire. The winds of war were starting to heat up the Balkans and it was time to go.

Kerassia, Turkey - The Ottoman Empire - Circa 1910

Last photo of Kerassia taken before the Earthquake.

Tthis was one of the stones that came tumbling down that sad day in Kerassia. That tragic Earthquake ruined the village but, on the other hand, it was the beginning of a new life for many survivors.

"I was thinking…..Vignettes of a Life Well Spent"

EULOGY TO HELEN

In the book of Ecclesiastics is written….
> *"For every thing there is a season,*
> *"A time to be born and a time to die"*

Helen Stratis Stavros was my Godmother and her presence was felt in my life from the moment I was born and will stay with me until the moment I die.

…She was there for me

My story is a personal testimonial to this gentle and beautiful lady but it reflects her values and her life.

In the depth of the vicious depression of the thirties, I was born under the most modest conditions practically in the front room of the Stratis family on Princeton Street in Somerville, Mass. It was not an easy birth and as the women tended to my Mother, I was put into the arms of my Godmother who soothed me and transmitted love.

…She was there for me

71

And several years later as a young boy of 7 or 8 with all the fears and insecurities of that age in a hostile world, my parents would take me to visit my Godparents from time to time after a long drive from Newport, Rhode Island. My Godmother would hug me at the door and usher me into the living room to the loving embrace of my Godfather sitting in the corner easy chair holding court over the elders and this blessed lady would place a straight back chair at the right hand of my Godfather for me to sit with him. She would keep an eye on me from the dining room doorway and just about every 10 or 15 minutes she would be offering me something to eat or drink. She made me feel wanted and important and I needed that.

...She was there for me

About 5 years later when I was 12 or 13, my Godfather decided it was time to teach me something about the finer things in life and my Godmother arranged a visit to a very ornate beautiful moving picture theatre on Washington Street in Boston. I can still remember that sweeping staircases, the fantastic chandeliers, the thick red carpet...it was ecstasy. And then she arranged for the three of us to go to dinner at one of the most exclusive restaurants in Boston...it was like being in the movies. That day I set my sights for life a little bit higher.

...She was there for me

It was a hot day at my College graduation but sitting there next to my parents were my Godmother and Godfather. They were so proud of me that even I had to start feeling good about myself.

...She was there for me

And in Boston a year later, the scene was repeated as I finished my Graduate studies.

...She was there for me

Then off to the military and foreign service

...She was there for me

Each step along the way as I labored at my profession, her infectious pride in my achievements made me believe more in myself.

...She was there for me

When I had my children and brought them to Florida to meet my Godmother.....she took them into her arms with that gentle unrestricted love.....she could see no imperfection and focused only on the good and the beautiful. The last time I saw my Godmother she was sitting on the sofa at Florence Spanolis' house and holding hands with my daughter Jaclyn commenting on her beauty and loving manner and totally disregarding the anomalies with which Jaclyn was born.

...She was there for me

Florence, Arthur and Connie honored her as the big sister she always was and their love and care knew no equal.

...She was there for them

Childless, some might say - NO, NO, a thousand times NO - look at all these nieces and nephews and all their children.

...She was there for them

And friends, each of you will remember this woman in a special and unique way that only you two shared in life.

...She was there for you

"THE GIFT OF GOD IS EVERLASTING LIFE"

Now, my Godmother is once again in the loving embrace of my Godfather, Peter, and she is with her parents, Nicola and Pagio, and with her brothers Sam and Ralph and with my parents and their other "patrioti" - I can hear the laughter and the stories - it is like Princeton Street déjà vu all over again.

There is a photo in my study that shows a group of villagers in the land of our origin, the village of Kerassia in Turkey on the European shore of the Sea of Marmara that was taken 86 years ago. Standing near the front is a beautiful 4 year old girl in a pretty dress - *my Godmother.*

Kerassia, Turkey   1910

We now have lost the pioneers in our family who ventured out bravely into this new world to give us all a special place in life. I will cry this day for our loss but I am also joyful. Jesus told us in the gospels "In my father's house there are many rooms, I go to prepare a place for you". And in one of these rooms when my time comes my Godmother will be waiting for me with a warm embrace and she will place a straight back chair for me to sit at the right hand of my Godfather and she will watch me from that doorway to the dining room to comfort me.

...She will be there for me.

June 5, 1996

74

"I was thinking…..Vignettes of a Life Well Spent"

FACE OF DEATH

How many times do we look into the Face of Death before we die? The answer is Three. And then after those three comes the final time we will look into that haunting Face of Death.

My first encounter with this evil face was in 1935 when I was five years old. It was a summer Thursday afternoon when my Dad had taken my brother John and me for a stroll onto Elm Street Pier off of Washington Street jutting out into Narragansett Bay in our hometown of Newport, Rhode Island.

Some men on the pier were fishing but most of the folks were just enjoying the sunny day. My father, Teddy, walked to the end of the pier to chat with some of the men and John was fooling around with other kids when I tripped on a loose plank at the edge railing, lost my balance and fell off the pier and sank at a point in the Bay that was probably not much deeper than about six feet of water. As I was being dragged below the water for the second time despite my desperate splashing to try to stay afloat, some passerby screamed out "Hey, there is a little kid drowning down here!" Within seconds my dad, Teddy, dove into Narragansett Bay to save me. Fully clothed and not even able to take the time to doff his hat, Dad swept me into his arms and swam with me in his embrace to shore. That was my first look into the Face of Death as reported in the Newport Daily News and the Newport Mercury:

75

Later in 1951 when I was in basic training at the Army base of Fort Dix, New Jersey, my name had fallen through the cracks when every guy in my unit was given leave to go home for either Christmas or for New Year's Day. No leave permission papers had been issued for me for the holidays. Feeling aggrieved, I decided to go AWOL after duty on Friday, December 28th, to spend the weekend at home and planned to return to the base for duty on Wednesday morning's reveille at 7 AM on January 2, 1952 so that my absence would not be discovered.

IN SAME REGIMENT — Newporters assigned to Company K, 47th Infantry Regiment, at Fort Dix, N. J., are Pvt. Edward J. Harrigan, left, and Pvt. Gregory T. Parkos. Harrigan is husband of Mrs. Margaret J. Harrigan of 5 Princeton street. Parkos is son of Mr. and Mrs. Theodore K. Parkos of 118 Bliss road.
(U. S. Army Photos)

It was a little bit risky because I knew that if I was not in the lineup on that morning, I would be charged with being AWOL and my appointment as a candidate for the Army's Counter Intelligence Corps would have been erased and I would be placed in line for assignment to an Infantry unit in Korea upon completion of my basic training. All went well during the few days that I was at home with my family and then on New Year's Day, I dashed off to get back to my base on time…from Newport I took the bus to Providence and then boarded the train for New York City's Pennsylvania Train Station where I changed trains to get to Bordentown, New Jersey, which was close to Fort Dix. I was just in time to get on a 9:30 PM train. As the train was leaving the station, the Conductor started calling out the next several stops on the schedule. As I heard him call out "Philadelphia" rather than "Bordentown" I realized that I was on the express train rather than the local route. Panicking, I grabbed my duffle bag and ran for the door which I was able to open enough to jump off the train. As I dropped spread out on the platform, I realized that I was only inches away from the end of the platform. Had my jump off the train been even just a second or two later, I would have fallen to the tracks and my death. Exhausted and shaking with fright, I picked myself up and was able to get on the midnight local train to Bordentown and was in the

76

lineup for reveille the next morning, a little beat-up but still alive after my second encounter with the Face of Death.

Some 25 years later, after visiting the Fram filter factory in Sao Paolo, Brazil, as President of CPL Corporation, the supplier of Urethane Filter Gasketing material to that company, I decided to take the weekend off and visit Rio de Janeiro before returning home to Rhode Island. It was 1975 and the weather was just perfect for hanging out and listening to Antonio Carlos Jobim's Bossa Nova music. Not much fun to be alone in that lovely setting but a lot better than not being there and alone.

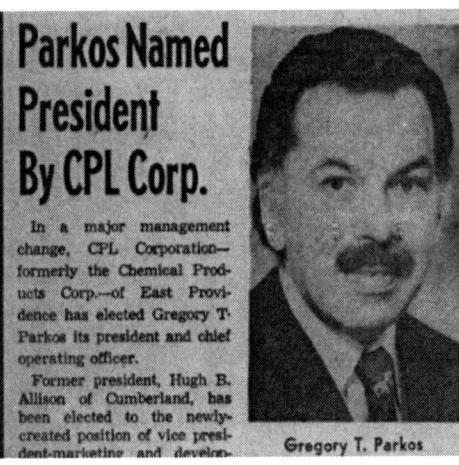

Parkos Named President By CPL Corp.

In a major management change, CPL Corporation—formerly the Chemical Products Corp.—of East Providence has elected Gregory T. Parkos its president and chief operating officer.

Former president, Hugh B. Allison of Cumberland, has been elected to the newly-created position of vice president-marketing and develop-

Gregory T. Parkos

On Monday morning I checked out of the Sheraton Rio Hotel overlooking Ipanema Beach. By the doorway of the hotel, I grabbed a taxi and told the driver that I was in a hurry to catch a flight and to waste no time getting me to the airport. The driver was eager to please and pushed his small automobile at a high rate of speed on the freeway to the airport largely exceeding even the craziest limits. About halfway to the airport, the cabdriver crashed into another vehicle and his taxi was just about totally demolished.,.it was a miracle the driver and I even survived. The driver got to his feet after extricating himself from the cab and then pulled me and my baggage out of the car before standing in the middle of the road to flag down a passing automobile to take me to the airport as quickly as possible. When I arrived at the airport an hour later, I realized that I had not paid him anything or even properly thanked him for his efforts to "get me to the airport on time." It all happened so fast that I did not even recall seeing the Face of Death that last time until much later.

Three times I have seen the Face of Death so there is nothing for me to do now but wait for our final meeting.

"I was thinking…..Vignettes of a Life Well Spent"

FACING JACK DEMPSEY

Jack Dempsey was the Heavyweight Boxing Champion of the World from 1919 to 1926 and I faced him three times in my life.

The first time I stood in a fighting ring facing the "Manassa Mauler" was in 1943 when I was a 13 year old boy being escorted by my Dad to shake hands with the Champ. The ring had been set up in the gymansium of De La Salle Academy in Newport and the event was a War Bond Drive in support of our troops in World War II. Jack Dempsey was a Commander in the U.S. Coast Guard and was traveling around the country selling War Bonds to help the war effort. He was a "Giant" and I was nervous until I saw him grasp my father's hand and then quickly turn toward me and "knuckled" my chin gently with his right hand all clenched up like a fighting fist. My Dad bought a War Bond

and I got punched by The Heavyweight Champion of the World.

Our second encounter was also a unique experience. The President of Rosbro Plastics Company, my boss Bert Brown, and I had just finished working the 1960 Toy Fair at the showrooms of Bert Coplon, our agent, at 200 Fifth Avenue in New York City where our products were being displayed. It was Friday night and March 11th, my birthday, so Bert invited me to have dinner as his guest at any place of my choice. It was going to be just Bert Brown and me, so I chose Jack Dempsey's Broadway Restaurant. As we approached the front door we could see through the window that Jack Dempsey was sitting in a booth right next to the front door. When we entered, the Champ rose to his feet to greet us and listened carefully as I told him the story of our first meeting. He took us to another booth and asked the waiter to set us up a round of drinks since as he put it "this guy and I were in the ring together during the war."

Some 30 years after our first meeting, I was with Jack Dempsey for the very last time. A friend of mine was marrying a young lady at the Westchester Country Club outside New York City and it was a very special and elegant event. Someone put a glass of Champagne in my hand as I entered the garden area where a small cluster of folks had gathered in a circle around someone in a wheelchair. The Grandfather of the bride invited me to join the group and began to introduce me to The Heavyweight Boxing Champion of The World Jack Dempsey sitting in that wheelchair and holding out his fighting right hand to greet me. When I told the Champ about our previous two meetings, he clinched his right hand and "knuckled" my cheek again with that symbol of who he was and will always be, "The Heavyweight Boxing Champion of The World."

"I was thinking…..Vignettes of a Life Well Spent"

FATHER'S DAY

Teddy Parkos was pleased with himself on this Friday morning as it looked like the job that he and Sam Stratis were painting would be done today and the $60 they would be paid was a handsome sum for just four days of work. The site was a beautiful Victorian style house with white shingles and a large lawn in front of a broad porch just around the bend from Harvard Square in Cambridge, not very far from where they lived in Somerville.

Upon their arrival the owner, Mrs. Collins, was on the porch and she asked Teddy if he would mind putting up her American Flag as she could not reach the bracket herself. With obvious enthusiasm Teddy raised the flag and even saluted it when he had finished. Mrs. Collins was just as happy and told Teddy that since the day was June 14th, it was Flag Day and she liked to fly the flag in memory of her son who was killed in France during the War. Teddy replied that he also has been in the War, served in France and had great admiration and love for his comrades who had died serving their country….and then, the tear in her eye turned into a smile and she was proud.

The day ended quickly and as they were being paid Mrs. Collins asked them if they could come back on the next morning and help her move some furniture and other items back into the bedrooms for which she would pay them some extra money. It took them just a few hours to do that task on the Saturday morning and Mrs. Collins handed them each a Ten dollar bill. They parted with joyful handshakes and pleasant thoughts.

When Teddy arrived home he could not stop talking about the happy events on the job and told Mary, his new bride of five months, that he was a very lucky guy and he wanted to celebrate. They planned a picnic for the next day which was a Sunday, June 16, together with their best friends Peter Stavros and Helen Stratis and a bunch of other friends and relatives.

The Sunday picnic was glorious and happy and when Teddy and Mary returned home that night they were exhausted but feeling great about each other and their life together. It had taken Mary a long time to get comfortable with married life as she was a very innocent bride but each special event like that particular day made the mating a lot easier.

Teddy was stretched out on their bed while Mary finished her nightly preparations and slid into bed. Starting to drift off to sleep, Teddy was awakened suddenly when his wife rolled over slipping her leg over his and whispered softly in his ear "Today is Father's Day and I want to have your child."

Just about Nine months later Mary gave birth to their first child.....conceived on Father's Day, June 16, in 1929 and born on March 11, 1930.....and he was named Gregory.

This is a photo of the father and son at Gregory's high school graduation 18 years later when Teddy was 50:

"I was thinking…..Vignettes of a Life Well Spent"

FIRED!

The City Hall Shoe Repair Shop on Broadway in Newport, R.I., was the only shoe shine parlor in that city to have electric shoe shine brushes and in 1941 at age 11, I became the youngest shoe shine boy on the stand where the other boys were 12 and 13 years old. There were 4 of us all together and we had a pecking order, the oldest kid got the first chair and so on down the line. I got the last chair to start which meant that at best I would get every fourth customer but more often than not, the first three chairs were not filled when the fourth customer came in so I was lucky to get one out of every five or six customers. Over time, I became the older shoe shine boy and was able to get one out of every three customers so everything worked out kept the job long enough. The tips were ours to keep which usually amounted to 5 cents or less per shine since the shoe shine cost 10 cents in those days. I remember Mr. Harry Horgan, one of the largest property owners in town, he came in every Sunday after church for one of us to shine his black lace-up shoes….the real trick was to shine his shoes without getting any polish on his white socks.

My pay amounted to $6.00 per week and I got a freshly laundered gray jacket every week. During the summer we worked from 9 a.m. to 6 p.m. during the week, until 9 p.m. on Saturday and only until 1 p.m. on Sundays. Winter hours were adjusted to give us time for school. I was certainly proud that I had that job and on the first day I worked I ran home during my lunch break wearing my gray jacket with pride to show it to my mother and hoping that the girls in the neighborhood would also get a glimpse of me at the same time…boy, did I look like a dandy or, at least, I thought I did. Payday was on Friday and my reward was a small coin envelope about 4 inches long and 2 inches wide with five crisp dollar bills rolled up inside together with three quarters, a dime, one nickel, and four pennies….$5.94. The missing 6 cents was a deduction for social security tax because now I was an honest to goodness wage earner as far as the government was concerned with my very own social security card issued at the age of eleven.

82

My first job had been at Ann's Hat Shop when I was nine and I had spent the time from age ten to eleven working on the streets as a shoe shine boy and newspaper hawker...but more about that at another writing.

After about a year or so a shoe shine boy, I was promoted to help with shoe repairs where I could help the craftsmen with a large order we had to re-sole and re-heel military work boots for the Marines who were stationed in Newport and training for the big war which had just started. I was feeling great about this new challenge when the owner, Mr. Tony Spirotis, a Greek American contemporary of my father, transferred me to an even more important job in his dry cleaning plant, the Valet Cleaners. This was a real factory with about 50 workers doing laundry and dry cleaning and pressing....I was really in the big time now and my salary had increased to $12.00 per week before those dreaded social security deductions, of course. In the beginning, my job was to brush the dirt from the cuffs but before long I was helping the girls in the plant who were washing the laundry in big tumblers and pressing the larger items on giant manglers with special pressing machines for shirts and so on. These were real women and I was wide eyed as they would flaunt there somewhat exposed chests and bodies accompanied by the toughest profanity I had heard to that time. I watched stealthily and listened rapturously to every word and sound. This was a helluva lot better than those mannequins at Ann's Hat Shop and I really liked the earthy girls of the laundry better than the fine ladies of the hat shop.

Soon I was helping with the stripping of the dry cleaning machines where we would empty the solvent saturated mud from the filters every Saturday morning and on occasion I would also help with manning a pressing machine in the press room. Gosh, I was doing a man's work and I was happy and proud...the rapture of the sound of manufacturing was music to my ears. Sometimes I would go to the small toilet that was in the factory, lock the door, and fantasize...oh, the joy of being a young boy in puberty ...for a split second, I really gushed with ecstasy.

And then, I opened the door and went back into the sweaty laundry room to my earthy goddesses with a little smile on my face for I had seduced one or more of them in my mind in that little toilet.

The time went by and the boss liked me for I was a hard worker and very respectful at all times. In 1943 when I was thirteen, my father decided to open a small restaurant and it was decided that everyone old enough in the family would work in his restaurant to insure our success. Thus it became necessary for me to resign my job at the Valet Cleaners and I had to tell Mr. Spirotis the news.

Haltingly, I began by explaining in my youthful way... "Mr. Spirotis, I have to give you notice because my father is going to open a restaurant and he wants me to be the dishwasher...."

As quick as a flash of lightening he thundered... "You don't have to give me any notice; I was going to fire you anyway." That ended my career as a shoe shine boy and cleaning plant worker.

God was angry! Some years later, Mr. Spirotis was bankrupt, his wife left him, and his oldest son was mentally distressed and unable to sustain himself. Personally, I think God may have overreacted to my treatment but who am I to judge God.

The real after-thought is an odd one for I did see Mr. Spirotis a number of times over the years and as my professional life unfolded, he extolled my virtues louder and louder to anyone who would listen and proclaimed that I was the best boy that ever worked for him. He had framed and mounted on the wall in his living space the canceled check of the very first paycheck issued to me when I worked in the cleaning plant...$ 11.88 (after that dreaded social security tax deduction of twelve cents)...and wanted everyone to look at it.

He was, after all, a good guy but his ego would not let a thirteen year old boy win an exchange.

Did I ever remind him that he fired me? Of course not! I cared about him and he was, after all, chairman of my fan club.

FIRST BORN CHILD

Every once in a while something happens that takes your breath away. It happened in Venice, Italy, on December 25, 1998 as I worshipped at the Greek Orthodox Cathedral there with my wife, Nadine, and my daughter, January.

It was fascinating to be attending services in Italy in a Greek community that had existed there for more than 500 years. But not strange since actually the Venetians had controlled Constantinople before its fall to the Turks and the beginning of the Ottoman Empire under which my parents were born.

The Church was designed in the classical European fashion with high chairs on each of the sidewalls and a large open space in the middle with no pews or chairs for the congregation. There were only about a dozen people in church but an Archbishop was presiding with two priests attending him and a small group of cantors that maybe numbered 3 or 4 and that was the total congregation.

The service was ornate because of the Archbishop and just as he turned to invite those in the congregation who were prepared to come forward and receive communion, I turned to January and asked her if she would join me. She took my right hand to her lips and kissed it with a plea for forgiveness. All of a sudden I was a little boy again bowing before my Grandfather and my Father asking for their forgiveness so that I could receive communion fully prepared.

With tears in my eyes and absolute joy in my heart, January and I approached the Archbishop and received the Eucharist as January called out her baptismal name "Panagiota" and I, having just heard my Mother's name, choked as I whispered "Gregorios". Redeemed, again! We are redeemed, again! My Mother in heaven has interceded, again!

"I was thinking.....Vignettes of a Life Well Spent"

FIRST BORN

It was cold and it was dark in the bedroom of the first floor tenement on Princeton Street in Somerville, Massachusetts on that Tuesday night in March. March 11th, as a matter of fact, just after 8 and the setting looked like a scene from a Shakespeare tragedy.

Three women hovered around Mary as she was trying to give birth to her first child. Sophia was there as the younger sister, Magdeline was there as someone who had given birth before, and Dialihti was there as the practiced midwife. They all lived in the neighborhood which was totally composed of families from the same little village in Turkey, Kirasia.

The men were upstairs in the second floor tenement which was the home of Nicola and Piagho Stratis and the focal point for all families on this street. Piagho was serving food and the men were celebrating the evolving event with raucous humor and loud laughter. Teddy, the proud father-to-be, was the center of attention as they drank ouzo with toasts of love and congratulations for the arrival of the newest member of the clan.

86

Grim was the scene in the bedroom for Mary had eaten with abandon during her pregnancy to get some relief from the day to day boredom that was her lot as the wife of the gay young blade who preferred to spend his time upstairs with the Stratis family rather than sit with his wife in their quiet and modest living quarters. The labor was coming very hard and the pain was causing her to gasp in shrieking cries that grew louder and louder with each contraction when all of a sudden a head started out of that throbbing womb. Within minutes the child was issued and Dialihti yelled out in a booming voice "It's a boy."

Dialecti was a large and strong woman with a firm manner in all things and she ordered Magdeline to go upstairs immediately and notify the father that he had a son.

Just as Magdeline was running out the front door, Dr. McCarthy was walking up the front steps to attend to the mother and child. He went directly to the bedroom, took the baby whose umbilical cord had been cut and knotted by Dialihti, and threw him onto a nearby towel thrusting the entire bundle into Sophia's arms. "Clean him up" he instructed and Sophia started to wipe the yellow globs from the newborn child. He was covered with fat and gunk from head to toes with splotches of blood throughout. The Doctor tended to Mary who was severely pained in giving this difficult birth as his most urgent mission and left the child to the care of the women.

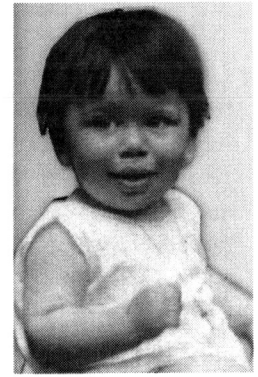

Teddy jumped up and danced in the middle of Paghio's kitchen in delight when he heard Magdeline shout out loud that he had a son as she ran into the room. The drinks and the bellows of good cheer upstairs lasted well into the night while the throbbing mother downstairs held her prized savior close to her heart.

Gregory was born March 11, 1930 and this is the photo taken one year later.

"I was thinking…..Vignettes of a Life Well Spent"

FIRST PEW / CENTER RIGHT

Almost no one ever sits there on a Sunday morning. It is the pew occupied by the most immediate family members of the deceased at every funeral at St. Spyridon's Church in Newport, Rhode Island.

I sat there for my Mother and Father and since I am the first born in my family, I pray that I will never have to sit there again…it is the worst seat in the house.

But who will sit there for me? My daughters, my wife, my sisters, my brother? Who will grieve for me? There is only room for four or five in that first pew and maybe deliberately so because there are so few we each leave behind that will miss us.

I do not fear death, at least not a kindly sort of death, as my life has been full and I have just about accomplished all that I needed to do and I now begin to prepare myself to journey forward. There is still a lot of repentance to get done and a lot of good to do, but I am on that road at this point in my life, November 17, 1997.

So long as anyone remembers me or my teaching, I shall be among the living and when those who might remember me are gone, so also am I finally gone…

That's it…there is no overtime in this game.

FORGIVE ME

" Συγχωρεσεμε ? "

The ritual was well known to us as young children even though we normally only performed it once a year. The hardest part was having to memorize the Greek word for "forgive me" which was a key component of the procedures we had to follow which also included long fasting.

On Thursday of Holy Week the adult congregation of St. Spyridon Greek Orthodox Church in Newport commemorated the Last Supper during the evening services.

But most of the young folks of the Church attended an earlier service during that day at which they received communion. To partake of this sacrament is one of the most holy things within the faith and one has to be properly prepared for it. The first step of this process is to erase the errors of your ways and to ask forgiveness for your faults from those within the family who are your seniors.

For me, that meant waiting at home for Dad to return from his having finished the night shift as a watchman at the City Yard on Long Wharf. Usually, that was about 8:30 in the morning and with guidance from my Mother, I would approach my Dad and take his right hand to my lips. With a kiss to his hand, I would repeat the memorized phrase asking for his forgiveness:

" Συγχωρεσεμε ? "

His hand would stroke my hair and then he would kiss my cheeks to signal his granting of my request for forgiveness. My brother and my sisters would take their turns to perform the same act of contrition. With the blessings of our father, we would then begin our walk to the church all together with our mother.

Along the way, about a block away from our tenement home on Thames Street, we made a stop at the Mahogany Bar to ask forgiveness from our grandfather who was the cook at that saloon.

It was the kind of bar that catered essentially to men and was generally off limits to women except for those lacking in moral values but definitely off limits without exception to youngsters like me. Consequently, I had to enter through the back door to visit my "Papou." Everyone in town knew my grandfather by that name which was the Greek nickname for a Grandfather. The few men who were at the bar that early in the day turned toward the little kitchen to watch me approach "Papou" and ask him in the same manner as I did my father, kissing his right hand and saying:

" Συγχωρεσεμε ? "

He grabbed me around the shoulders and lifted me to his face where his grisly beard would scratch my face as he kissed me with his forgiveness. The joy was so great that it overcame the scratchy beard.

Within a half hour we were at the church steps which we ascended and entered the front doors to receive our communion.

At the last moment before approaching the altar, I turned to my Mom and whispered softly as I reached up and embraced her with both arms and felt tears coming down her face as she held me tightly:

" Συγχωρεσεμε ? "

Nothing more needed to be said…

I had been forgiven and it was time for me to take the spoon of Holy Communion while the Priest prayed for me with the words:

"Taking communion is the servant of God, Gregory, in the name of the Father, and the Son, and the Holy Spirit, Amen!"

"I was thinking…..Vignettes of a Life Well Spent"

FRUIT ON THE WALL

It was the house on John Street in Newport as I remember it…it was the home of Theos Dialegmenos and Kyria Eleni and their two sons, Dean and Vios.

Theos is the Greek word for Uncle and Kyria is the Greek word for Madame. This couple was the elders of our clan in America as Theos had been educated somewhat in Constantinople and was one of the first to come to the United States in about 1911. He was respected by all because he had been educated and he carried himself with the regal bearing of a leader.

His first home in Boston had become the landing spot for all new immigrants from the village of Kerasia, Turkey, from 1912 until the early twenties when immigration stopped. When the depression proved especially difficult in the big city of Boston, they moved to Newport, Rhode Island where making a living was a little easier during the early thirties. The Parkos family followed a few years later.

Back to the house on John Street. My parents would take us on special days to visit their family and I was always awestruck by two prints in the dining room framed in rather large oval frames and glass covered. The picture was of exotic tropical fruit like I had never seen before or ever expected to see again. There were bananas, small and perky, and there were cherries, round and plump, and there were melons, large and succulent. I dreamed of paradise there and I wondered if such a place existed and if I would ever eat of that fruit.

The hunger of the eyes is greater than any hunger of the stomach and I have not forgotten that fruit although the meager meals of those times has long since been forgotten.

"I was thinking…..Vignettes of a Life Well Spent"

GASSED!

What were the words he heard as he stood there slumped against the blood drenched earthen wall that lined both sides of the trench? Was it "Gas—Gaas--Gaaas—Pass it on." As Erich Maria Remarque wrote in *All Quiet on the Western Front* or was it the words in Wilfred Owen's sad poem *Dulce et Decorum Est* which cried out "Gas! Gas! Quick, boys!"

Whatever the words, he grabbed his mask but it was late…and Dad was gassed.

"Teddy, you lucky bastard…you only got a sniff of that mustard gas" the steward assured him as he cleaned his eyes of small painful blisters, "and your blindness is only temporary." What the steward could not see was that the lung damage was to linger for many years as a chronic illness for this energetic young man. He was offered a small disability pension and was treated at the Chelsea Military Hospital for a while after the war. But he had a life to live, and he put that behind him so that he could move on. A few years later He gave up the pension and refused any further medical treatment. But he would not forget those days in the trenches.

"Gassed" by John Singer Sargent

The story began earlier. It had been a tiring weekend for this young immigrant boy who had arrived in Boston only 5 years earlier from Turkey to join his brother, Gregory. The restaurant in Park Square where he worked in the kitchen had been quite busy and Theodosios was happy to have this Monday off. It was the regular day that he had off each week but today something special was in the air. The date was April 2, 1917 and there was a lot of chatter on each street corner about something important happening but he did not know exactly what they were talking about.

Later that day, as he walked up to Highland Avenue in Somerville and headed for the bakery near Union Square, he saw the Boston Evening Transcript at the newsstand. It was marked in bold letters with the word "EXTRA" and then an equally bold headline "WILSON ASKS WAR DECLARATION" with a sub-headline that called out "CALLS FOR 500,000 MEN".

When Theodosios arrived at the bakery, he asked his compatriot from the little Turkish-Greek village where he was born: "Hercules, What does this mean?" The answer was clear and unambiguous: "Theodosios, they want young men to fight the Germans and they will automatically make these volunteers American citizens for serving in this war." That was all he needed to hear and the next day, Theodosios offered himself for service in the American Expeditionary Forces in the First World War.

93

At the Boston Army Base where he enlisted, a byproduct of his joining the United States Army was his new name…Theodore K. Parkos….and his nickname would be "Teddy."

Teddy Parkos was one of the 500,000 men that President Woodrow Wilson had asked for and his first assignment was Fort Riley, Kansas, the absolute center of the geographic 48 United States, where he attended the Cooks and Bakers school.

After finishing his training at Fort Riley, this 20 year old young man volunteered to transfer to a combat unit with the United States Second Cavalry to prepare for service in Europe with the American Expeditionary Forces (AEF). And very soon he was at Fort Ethan Allen in Vermont for intensive combat training with Troop G of the 2nd Cavalry Regiment.

He was happy as hell for now he was a real American training with his comrades. The Argentinian horses they were using were tall and had been selected because of their stature for combat use.

Ft Ethan Allen - November 17, 1917   Mounted Cavalry

94

The training was arduous but he enjoyed the camaraderie of his fellow troopers.

In April 1918 Troop G, Second Cavalry landed in France in the Toul Sector...

...and they gained the unique distinction as the only American Cavalry on horseback to reach the firing line.

They fought in Aisne-Marne offensive in July 18 – August 6, 1918, when the American First and Second Divisions smashed in the West face of the German Marne Salient at Soissons.

And the Oise-Aisne offensive, August 18 – September 11 1918.

The greatest commendation was gained by Troop G for its part in the reduction of the St. Mihiel Salient, September 12 – 16, when they were attached to the American First Division of the Fourth Army Corps, making the main effort of the American First Army in France.

General Pershing massed six Divisions on an eighteen mile front, the 1st Division jumped off by passing Mont Sec, which the French had assaulted for years in vain, and reached the line Heudicort-Nosard. Here the Americans passed through the forest of La Belle Oziere, Nonsard, and Vigneulles, scouted the open country as far as Heudicourt Creue, and Vigneulles, eventually advancing to St. Maurice, Woel, Jonville, pursuing the enemy, fighting his rear guard, capturing numerous prisoners, forcing deployment and delaying his retreat, in fact, doing everything that so small a force could accomplish.

This action was followed by the final Allied offensive, the Meuse-Argonne, September 26 to November 11, 1918, with the Second Cavalry being attached to the American 35th Division, the left flank of eight Divisions then attacking between the Meuse River and the Argonnes Forest. The plan of the American First Army was to bypass the strong points of Montfaucon and Romagne on both sides and seize the high ground at Barricourt with a converging effort, which would shatter all German positions before Sedan.

The 35th Division spearheaded the assault on the left, in an engagement where the troops of the Second Cavalry "during the six days battle at Vauquois, Bois de Rossigny, Quvrage D'Aden, Cheepy, Charpentry, Baulny, Bois de Montre Beau, and Exermont from September 26 to October 2, 1918, accomplished their tasks with fearlessness, courage and disregard of danger and hardship." (Quote by P. E. Traub, Major General, Commanding 35th Division.)

The Second Calvary was also commended for the operation North of Busancy and in Beaumont from November 3 – November 6, patrolling the entire front of the Division sector in advance of the Infantry which resulted in military information of great value, riding into machine gun and artillery swept areas time and time again and drawing fire in successful efforts to aid the advance of the Infantry by locating machine gun nests and enemy parties digging in.

With the Germans driven across the Meuse at Sedan the Armistice was signed on November 11, 1918 marking the cessation of hostilities. The Second Cavalry remained with the Army of Occupation in Germany until August 1919 when it returned to Fort Riley, Kansas, and Teddy Parkos then came home in triumph.

"I was thinking.....Vignettes of a Life Well Spent"

GENERATIONS

"One generation passeth away, and another
generation cometh: but the earth abideth for ever"
....Ecclesiastes

At a glance you can see 6 generations sail by your range of vision and when you try to catch your breath, the cascade of continuing names strikes you with a clear message of "*Continuum.*"

Since the beginning of Byzantium, maybe a thousand generations ago, Byzantine Greeks have been naming their children in honor of predecessors to continue the remembrance of loved ones. The lack of written records allow the recall of only a few of past generations now so we only have this short story to tell this day as we talk of Panagiota and Styliani over time.

During the summer of 1883 in the little village of Kerassia, bordering on the European side of the Sea of Marmara in the Ottoman Empire, a young lady about 20 years old named Panagiota married Ioannis Gianopoulos. There our story begins with the first generation of our memory...a woman named *Panagiota.*

Less than a year later, in 1884, a daughter was born to Panagiota and she was named *Styliani* to begin the second generation. The family prospered with their crops of fruit for the tables of Constantinople always in demand.

Even before she reached the age of 20, Styliani caught the eye of a suitor named Stergios but his pleas for her hand in marriage were turned away by her family since he did not have an equal status to her in the community. Not to be denied his love, Stergios was able to join with her in their mutual love to conceive a child so that the family would have to accept their marriage. The child was named *Panagiota* to honor her grandmother...and thus the third generation came to be in 1908.

99

A major earthquake in 1912 caused the village to be destroyed. Panagiota voyaged to America, where within 6 years she lost her revered mother, Styliani, in the Spanish Flu Pandemic of 1918. She survived the very difficult years of her youth, married a dashing young man named Theodore and began her own family. Her first daughter in 1936, was named *Styliani* by this Panagiota to honor her mother and to mark the fourth generation in this tale.

The continuum went on, when the new Styliani married a young man named Thomas and they also began their own family. Her youngest child was born in 1975, and the baby was named in her grandmother's honor as *Panagiota*, and so began the fifth generation in this unbroken chain.

This Panagiota married a loving partner named Joseph and God granted them another generation, when their new child came into the family this past week. Panagiota honored her own mother by naming the baby *Styliani*. Separate and apart from the cycle of alternating names, another daughter of the fourth generation Styliani, Leah, also named her daughter Styliani within the sixth generation.

Let it be recorded in Heaven and on Earth this gift to our family…..six generations of alternating honored names.

"So long as one is remembered by name they continue to live in spirit within our family and shall never leave us."

….Gregory T. Parkos

October 5, 2005

GIFTS

God has been good to me.

I am rich in family, as well as love and the material things of life on this earth….much more than I deserve but I am very thankful for them all.

The one thing that I cannot gift my children is the hardships of life that lead to all of these good things that surround me now.

Born in a tenement with the rent unpaid and depending on the favor of others for the food that was on our table, I had the greatest gift of man…a father who was proud to have me and a mother who adored me. That legacy made everything possible for me.

What can I give my children that is comparable….certainly the same pride and adoration with many more material things thrown in but how do I give them the hardships so necessary to build the will to succeed and sensitivity to people less well off?

Perhaps…just maybe, when they are faced with the dilemmas of life on questions of choice regardless of whether the matter is social or commercial, they will let the spirit of their father enter into their heads for just a few moments before they make the decision…..then, maybe I will be able to gift them with the benefits of the hardships that I could not give them under the Christmas tree.

"I was thinking…..Vignettes of a Life Well Spent"

GOOD INTENTIONS

Some of the most evil things in this world have been caused by good intentions. To see the awful agony of the derelicts and homeless on the boardwalk of Venice Beach made me wonder about what the politically lite thought they were accomplishing when they freed the inmates from mental institutions in the 60's to allow them free entry into society. Each different face that I saw with its ugly contortions and devastating physical derangement made me angrier and angrier that the consequence of this great liberal plan was an enslavement of mind and body much more severe and unforgiving than the institutions and for these victims, death was perhaps the only antidote to their sickness.

..and then I turned onto Main Street in Santa Monica and Venice and cast my eyes upon the splendid bodies and faces of the California Gods and Godesses in their thirties and forties and said to myself,,there are good things here also. The beautiful people and the pretty shops turned my mind to a scene I remember from last night and a scene I remembered from 50 years ago...

When January touched her Mother last night in that special way that can only exist between two people who are the closest to each other of any human beings on this earth, I remembered how I also held my Mother and cried and laughed with her because she was the closest person in the world to me until her death and the birth of my first child which happened within a 90 day period as if God said..."I need your best friend now but I'll give you a new best friend for the rest of your life".

There is something of a connection in my thoughts today between the hopeless and the loved. A person should honor the love of closeness more than anything in the world because without it, the heart is a lonely hunter. When the heat of disagreement rises, touch one another gently but definitely and hold on to each other through the angry words and the tears and then into the smiles and the laughter of relief because , once again, you have found that you are the closest two people on the face of the earth. God has been good to me and my life has been well spent...June 20, 1994.

"I was thinking…..Vignettes of a Life Well Spent"

HAPPY 18TH BIRTHDAY

January 1, 1996

To my January:

There have been many passions in my life such as sports, work, art, loves, music, literature, knowledge, wisdom, exploration, people and just plain living...but not any of these nor, indeed, not all of them lumped together begin to even approach the passion I have for you and the gratitude I feel that you are in my life.

It was March of 1977 and I had just passed my 47th birthday when you were conceived...truly a "love child"...and I began the bond with you that is mine to keep eternally. You entered where no one had ever been before and you took control of that portion of my heart that still explodes with pride whenever I hear you say "Daddy". With you in my heart, I never again felt alone.

On the 18th anniversary of your birth, I think about the little baby that looked at me first. You never saw anything or anyone before you looked straight at me and I could see in your eyes the miracle that was you.

God has been good to me and his best gift was my January.

Remember me always and I will keep you in my special heart forever.

To your father...you are love and you are loved.

HAPPY DAY

"It was the best of times." The Parkos family of Newport, Rhode Island, had just finished their happiest Christmas and it was now evening time on December 25, 1944. 14 years old and relishing with delight the Western Flyer Bicycle that was my special Santa gift.

The four Parkos kids received special gifts that year because our family was blessed with good rewards from the family business, the Supreme Lunch. My brother John at 13 years old and I worked every day at the restaurant, full time in the summers when we were not in school and part time after school the rest of the year. Dad and Mom, of course, worked full time all year round. The War had brought many young folks to Newport for Naval training and the family business thrived.

John and I crawled into our small bed that night filled with great feelings of joy. Our room was actually like a large closet adjacent to and accessible only through our parents' bedroom. While we whispered to each other the happiness of life that night, we also heard Mom and Dad talking to each other in muted voices rather than just falling asleep as they usually did when they went to bed together. We listened for a little bit but could not hear what they were saying clearly and just gave up with no more effort to catch on to their discussion. Earlier that day, I had heard my Dad expressing his concerns about the news broadcasts that were reporting from Athens that the insurrection by the Greek Communists was still raging and that Winston Churchill from Great Britain had gone there to try and end the conflict.

Not really understanding what that news meant, I was stunned and afraid to listen to my Dad's fears just as I was when the Japanese bombed the Americans at Pearl Harbor three years earlier.

Anyway, I just turned over and fell asleep next to my brother John and I could hear my folks talking to each other softly. It felt good to know that my parents were lovers also. I had heard their soft sounds from time to time as bedtime came for John and me and their joy was blissful.

Nine months later the youngest of the Parkos Kids joined the family in the common sense of the word, but I knew better. My baby sister, Elaine, actually joined our family on that Christmas night in 1944 when my Dad planted his seed in my Mom.

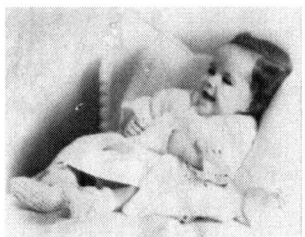

The pregnancy had frightened my Mom because she felt she was too old at age 36 to bear a child but my Dad was delighted that the whole universe would be able to testify to his virility. I thought it as a little embarrassing that now that I was coming into my young manhood, my Mother would be walking around with a big belly carrying a baby child. So, I pretended that it was not really happening. However in September of 1945, that pretense just got washed away because the baby Elaine was in our arms and The Parkos Kids became an intimate band of five siblings to this day. Soon we will part but our time together has been long and fruitful.

Mom's life started to turn into an accelerated rate of happiness as time went on after Elaine's birth. Her first cousin Danny, who was like a brother to her, and her brother Danny came back from the War battered but unbeaten and each of them had been a true hero, cousin Danny in Italy and France, and brother Danny in Burma. In August of 1945 they were back in Newport to join their "sister" as she delivered her fifth child.

With the start of the new year of 1946, both Cousin Danny and Brother Danny were starting their own families with boys on the way. And her sister, Sophia, was also growing her own family.

To top it all off, Dad decided to buy his first family home and settled on a beautiful piece of property at the bottom of Bliss Road which property is still within our family as the residence of Elaine and her family. It was almost the final sense of joy for Mary who never in her life had ever envisioned that she would own a home having lived in rented tenements for so many years.

Dad started calling his newest little girl by the nickname "Peaches" because her face was aglow with the soft plush color of that fruit and to express his own delighted sense of having another little darling daughter. The family was now complete with Mom and Dad and the Parkos Five Kids and Dad started to think about how he could express his sense of fulfillment and honor his friendship with so many people from his past and present.

Elaine's baptism had been delayed because of Dad's pursuit of a unique way to express his happiness in life. Finally it was decided to set Sunday, July 14th of 1946 as the date of the Christening and a large celebration was planned at our new home in Newport for their friends and relatives.

It was a grand event.

The sun was large and bright early that Sunday morning.

As the family prepared to depart for St. Spyridon Church for the Christening, the cars from Somerville and Arlington and Watertown began to pull up to the curb on the Fenner Avenue side of the house. The smile on Mom's face grew wider and wider with each new arrival and Dad's laughter and joy became louder and happier as he greeted each one from every car.

There were so many guests and friends of the family that the church was filled for the Baptism of Elaine, my Dad's "Peaches." Father Theodore, the Priest, proclaimed it the largest Christening he had ever performed and he was happy to see them all. So happy, that his welcoming comments lasted longer than any other sermon he had ever given.

The reception was in the back yard of the new Parkos home and the party continued hour after hour and not anyone wanted to leave, ever.

It was a "Celebration of Arrival."

The "Happy Day" they prayed for all their lives had finally arrived:

They were proud Americans.
They owned a home of their own.
They owned a business of their own.
They, together, had achieved success.
They had a healthy and happy family.
They had many loving friends and relatives.
They loved each other and their five children.

Mark it well in your memory....here they were on this Sunday, this July 14, 1946 that marked the happiest day in the lives of Teddy and Mary Parkos.

In 1947, the only photo of the entire Parkos family together ever taken commemorated their pride and joy in one another.

We lost our Dad ten years after the happiest day in his life at the very early age of 58.

Mom continued to love and enjoy her family until her departure some thirty two years after the happiest day in her life

The Five Parkos Kids continue to celebrate that "Happy Day."

"I was thinking…..Vignettes of a Life Well Spent"

HOT SHOT

I just heard that Peggy died. Just a week short of a birthday anniversary…was it 81 or 82, I can't remember but I do remember when I met her. It was 1955 in Athens and I was in my prime.

The word circulated around the U.S.A. government offices that Greg Parkos was a hot shot agent hustling around the borders surrounding Greece on the edge of doing something crazy like slipping into Albania to get a high level defector out or enticing a friend of a friend to seduce the chief of police in Sofia, Bulgaria into defecting. There were all kinds of stories more fiction than fact but I certainly did nothing to deflate the representation.

My work was well known. The one agent that was always anxious to be "on the road" rather than the sweet life of Athens. My superiors may have disliked my cavalier attitude but they sure did relish taking credit for my achievements. But when I was in Athens, that was another story and my misadventures were well known in the gossip circles of "happily-married, family-oriented, gentility that made up the super structure of our government services".

The story of An American Lady (no names need be used) tells it all. After I had been on assignment for about a half year, my Country Chief was assigned a new Administrative Assistant from Washington, An American Lady reported to be a career foreign service staff member and not a bad looker. Since I was in Athens at the time, I volunteered to meet her at the airport and welcome her to our station by seeing that she got to her hotel and was aware of the procedure for her to come to work the next day. The arrival greeting went well…I behaved nicely with a little bit of charm but no syrupy fussing over her. She was happy and comfortable.

From time to time when I would come back from the road to Athens, I would spend a little time flirting with An American Lady just because that was my nature and not because I had any real interest. She was a cold fish in my book....tall, thin and had a swell swish to her walk which would have turned me on but she also had a bit of a fish look to her mouth that I could not overcome as I considered the prospect of reeling her in. Therefore, I did not invite her to participate in our evening soirées.

But the Gods were not good to me on this one. It just so happened that one evening several of us were invited to a small embassy party and An American Lady turned out to be the least unattractive of the free participants so I spent a little extra time with her and consequently she asked if I would escort her home. On our way to her residence, she suggested that if I were a gentleman that I should invite her to my apartment for a nightcap since she had heard that I had a great apartment in Kolonaki. Silly me, not knowing an alternative...we went to my place. She had a drink in the living room and when I went to refresh her drink, she was able to maneuver into my arms and we were in a passionate kiss. It didn't work. My instincts about her fish like mouth blocked my emotion and I could not go on. She tasted like a shark so I had no interest.

When I told An American Lady that I did not have an interest in going on, she demanded to know why I refused her only since I was known to be quite generous about my affections for so many other girls and especially the Greek girls that worked in our offices.

When I told her that it was not true but rather just fancy stories that people made up about me, she demanded that I must make love to her or she would not leave that night.

The next morning when she awakened on my living room sofa after spending a lonely night without my presence, she did not speak a single word and I took her to her residence. It was the weekend.

On Monday morning, I left Athens to get back into the field and when I came back a few weeks later. The office was in a state of disaster. It seems that An American Lady became so angry at my rejecting her that she despised all Greeks and was being especially cruel to the locals who worked in the office. It had become an impossible situation and she had to go…and I was the culprit.

My Country Chief called me in and demanded to know what I had done to her. He did not find the story too comforting but because he desperately needed me in the field, he accepted the situation and ordered me to absolutely stay away from his new Administrative Assistant.

An American Lady was shuffled off to Hong Kong to take up an assignment that had been scheduled for Georgia Dent Robinson and Mrs. Robinson with her 6 year old daughter was posted to Athens to fill the open slot.

My orders were clear… "Do not go anywhere near her."

A southern belle and pretty neat looking at that….maybe in her thirties…nice figure…nice style…looking good…and Peggy was her nickname. I hadn't seen one like that for a long time…but, the words were ringing in my ears… "Do not go anywhere near her."

So I went back out into the field with my trusty bodyguard, driver, and interpreter Mario Scrivanos from Romania who hated the Communists with a deep passion for they had confiscated his shipping fleet and he had to escape with practically nothing. Mario was about 55 years of age and had within the past few years married a 25 year old Danish girl who worked at one of the International Associations in Athens…a fascinating couple...Mario spoke Romanian, French, Greek, and lousy English; whereas his wife spoke Danish, French, and almost perfect English….visiting them was great fun, they spoke to each other in French, Mario spoke to me in Greek, and I spoke to his wife in English...a three ring circus.

That particular trip was to Ioanina the closest large city to the Albanian border and we stayed in the region for a couple of weeks doing something or other. Each morning, Mario and I would sit on a sidewalk café, I would have a cup of coffee and Mario would eat eggs and chicken livers with a small glass of Mavrodaphene seet dessert wine, a meal he defended explaining to me that because of the age difference with his wife he needed that food to build his male power. It must have worked for soon, she was carrying his child.

Eventually, we got back to Athens and before I was in the office long enough to say my sweet things to all the ladies at their desks Peggy sent her secretary to ask me if I would have coffee with her. Damn it. I guess no-one had told her to stay away from me but I was soon to learn that she did know about the previous episode.

Coffee was on the roof of our office, the Tameion building in the center of Athens overlooking the Acropolis with the Parthenon on top. It was a priceless view and as we sipped coffee I just knew that Peggy had targeted me as the forbidden fruit and she wanted a taste.

The story line was that she needed a maid and that she had been told that I had many friends around the country and that I could arrange to get her a country girl from one of the villages to live with her and her daughter, Gayle. I agreed to take her to Tripoli the following Sunday to meet my friend Bill Clepas who owned the biggest hotel in that area who would arrange for her needs. Bill had been deported from Chicago in the early thirties when he was one of Al Capone's boys. He was an important ally of mine.

As we traveled back to Athens, we stopped at the tomb of Agamemnon for some sightseeing and then to Nafplion for dinner before I returned her to the bedroom of her Villa in Kifissia. The next morning I took her to breakfast at the American Club nearby and …Thus the Peggy and Greg affair started.
How it unfolded, developed and ended is yet another story to be told….maybe sometime!

"I was thinking.....Vignettes of a Life Well Spent"

HOW INSENSITIVE!

Was it the sixties…so hard to remember, the years have been long and the memory has been tormented by the passage of those long years…but that evening is remembered as clearly today as it was then.

New Orleans, on Bourbon Street, at a small bar named Villa Rosa…..in the early morning hours somewhere about an hour or two after midnight, sitting in the lounge with a Studio Grand Piano as my table while sipping from a glass of Absente with Peggy beside me. It had been a long and deadly evening and I was in the depth of my personal melancholy when the Chanteuse playing the piano started to sing…

> *"How Insensitive*
> *I must have seemed*
> *When she told me that she loved me."*

I remembered the song as one that Jobim had written for his new style of Samba called the Bossa Nova and my ears perked up as I began to feel the beat of the slow and smooth music blend…

> "How unmoved and cold
> I must have seemed
> When she told me so sincerely."

This song, this sentiment caught the essence of my sad state of mind as I sat there numbed by the alcohol but not enough to be unaware of the depth of my despair at the situation I had trapped myself into…

> *"Why she must have asked*
> *Did I just turn and stare in icy silence."*

And then I knew the answer only too clearly in my mind as the lyrics continued…

> *"What was I to say*
> *What can you say when a love affair is over."*

113

While I sat there and resolved that it was time to tell Peggy that it had ended and I had to straighten out this mess that I had created for the two of us, the singer continued with her song...

"Now she's gone away
And I'm alone with the memory of her last look
Vague and drawn and sad
I see it still
All her heartbreak in that last look."

To this day, I remember the difficult ending for us and the tragic musical tune being sung...

"How she must have asked
Could I just stare in icy silence."

And in my prayers I still ask whether I was fair and kind in what I did that night as I hear the last few words...

"What was I to do
What can one do when a love affair is over."

This "Love Affair" ended that night but it would be many years later before the legal arrangement of our marriage would be terminated and Peggy was taken care of for the rest of her life in material things but I am sorry to say that she never found the passion of a "Love Affair" again.

"I was thinking…..Vignettes of a Life Well Spent"

I DO

This writing by January M. Parkos was included in the program of the wedding of her father to Nadine in 1996:

I DO

The last spark of life shines through
and all I can think about is you.

When all life comes to a final spot
and the corpses begin to smell and rot.

When light as we know it has come and gone
and all that was present in our life does
dawn.

Then all I'll know and love so true
will begin and end with the words I do.

I do, oh what a lovely pair
without whom my life would be despair.

For never have I seen so lovely as two
than you and me in the words I do.

January M. Parkos
Los Angeles, '93

115

"I was thinking…..Vignettes of a Life Well Spent"

IL MARQUIS DI VENEZIA L'AMERICA

Arriving in Milan in the fall of 1982 after a long flight from Los Angeles, my driver took me directly from the airport to the Hotel Principe di Savoia at the Plaza de Republica…my favorite place in that city and one of the most elegant  hotels in the world. It was to be a quiet night of rest.

After a very short nap that afternoon, I decided to spend a little time in the Giardino d'Inverno Bar just off the lobby of the hotel:

The Giardino d'Inverno was an elegant, quiet corner at cocktail time to enjoy a relaxing moment in the evening. When the waiter brought me a martini, I caught the sight of slight trim gentleman in Tuxedo dress being joined at a small table across from me by a stunningly beautiful young woman. The whole scene was enhanced by discreet melodies from the piano and each sip from my glass just added to the feeling of mellowness I was feeling being there.

I heard the jingle of a small bell and then watched a bellman from the lobby walking through the bar with a hand held sign indicating that he had a message for a person entitled Il Marquis di Verona.

The gentleman in Black Tie sitting with the pretty lady raised his hand to signal to the Bellman for the message which he read very quickly, scribbled a reply on it, and then returned his attention to his beautiful companion. The girl moved closer to him and I was envious.

Ricardo, my driver, picked me up the next morning to take me to the Riva Yacht Company in the town of Sarnico adjacent to Lago Gardo. It was part of the Lake Country of Italy bordering Lake Como and Switzerland where I was to perform my quarterly review of this business as the Group Executive of the Marine Division of Whittaker Corporation.

The guy who ran Riva was named Gino Gervasoni and he was a fascinating fellow that had been

117

nicknamed "El Commandatore." Technically, it was a title that was bestowed only by decree of the President of Italy but that did not bother us very much.

The Riva Yacht Company made boats for the very wealthy people of the world and it was a delightful duty to serve as Chairman of that company within my duties at Whittaker during those years.

Typically we would spend a few hours reviewing the financial results of the company which were always quite good, and then we would launch one of our newest boats to take us to lunch on a small island in the middle of the lake. This was the time when we would discuss strategies.

Lunch would begin with liquid alcoholic refreshments which set the stage for a wonderful seafood meal and lots of refreshing Italian white wine. Concluding with a sweet plate and some excellent local Grappa to finish the meal, these luncheon discussions were so productive that there was no further need to talk about business.

This gave me the opportunity to ask Gino "How does one become a Marquis in Italy?" and then went on to explain to him what I had witnessed the night before at the hotel bar.

His response was very direct and unemotional. We had become good friends so we treated each other with a little bit of humor all the time, but never losing our respect for each other.

How did he explain this anointment of hierarchal title? Let me use his exact words"

"First, Gregorio, you go to a printer.
Then your write down what you want him to print on your card.
And, after that, you present your newly printed card to everyone.
That is how you become a Marquis."

Following his trusted advice, I present you with my calling card and await your appropriate use of my self-given title:

Gregory T. Parkos
"Il Marquis di Venezia"

420 Carroll Canal
Venice, California 90291, U.S.A.

Email: gregparkos@aol.com
Website: www.gregparkos.com

Tel: 310-827-7667
Fax: 310-827-8889
Cell: 310-869-4732

A few months later, I returned to the Principe di Savoie and the Front Desk referred me to the Concierge who handed me an envelope addressed to "Il Marquis di Venezia l'America." Enclosed was a ticket to attend the opening performance of a new opera at La Scala from my friend El Commandatore Gino Gervasoni.
Throughout this visit, I was constantly addressed as "Il Marquis" by all the staff. It is good when warm humor prevails over cold solemnity.

ILLEGAL

My Mother was an Illegal Immigrant!

Mary (Panagiota) Diomandes was 4 years old when she entered the United States of America in 1912 and she was a stowaway on board the ship traveling with her parents and grandmother, who were legally listed on the ship's manifest.

A stowaway, not because of any political or criminal purpose, but because her family did not have enough money to pay for her ticket and she was small enough to be passed into the country almost like a non-entity bustling within the skirts of her mother and grandmother.

Some 40 years after her illegal entry, my Father, who had been a citizen of the United States since shortly after his service in the American Army during World War I, engaged a prominent immigration attorney named something like "Zucor" in Providence, Rhode Island, to clean up her record so that she could apply for naturalization.

The attorney had to prove by some piece of evidence that Mary had been in the United States every year since her arrival. He used things like school documents, birth certificates of her children, testimony of citizens, census records, marriage certificate, church records and so on to establish that she had lived within this country for the previous 40 years since her illegal entry in 1912.

After this successful endeavor, the Parkos family celebrated a very quiet and emotional formal naturalization of their Matriarch.

My Mother loved this country with all her heart and soul and was proud to have died a "Legal Immigrant."

Remember this when you judge those who continue to search for the Glory, Happiness, and Opportunities of being an American.

"I was thinking…..Vignettes of a Life Well Spent"

IMAM BALDI IN CALCUTTA

Damon S. Diomandes was an American Guerrilla trained to lead Kachin Tribesmen behind the Japanese lines in Burma as part of the elite O.S.S. Detachment #101 during World War II. "Dan" had joined the Army in January of 1942 immediately after the bombing of Pearl Harbor

by the Japanese and after a short stint at the Cook and Baker's school in Fort Riley, Kansas, he was selected and volunteered for special training as a member of this unique special force. Their exploits are well documented in the annals of history but there are many little stories about them that still elude the record books. This is one of those tales.

In the middle of those war years, "Dan" was training in Calcutta before he was parachuted into Burma for his mission. A special session included an overview of the Japanese positions in Burma by Paul Cushing Child, an American who worked with the OSS designing war rooms in the China-Burma-India Theater of Operations.

Paul had lived in France for a number of years before the war and was regarded a connoisseur of fine cuisine. When they took a break from the briefing sessions, Paul and "Dan" talked about their backgrounds and discovered that they both had an interest in food and cooking. Very quickly they developed a friendship based upon their mutual experience in the culinary arts as well as their passions in the war effort.

When Paul learned that "Dan" came from a family that had its origins in Turkey, he insisted that they prepare a meal that evening from the Ottoman tables called "Imam Baldi," which "Dan" had learned to cook from Aunt Irene who had raised him. They scratched up some eggplants and myriad other special vegetables, so they could prepare this rather unique dish which was named "The Imam Faints" because tradition has it that the ruler of the Ottomans fainted when he first tasted this dish.

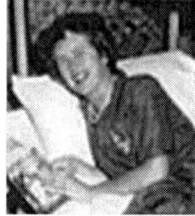Their guest at dinner that night in Calcutta was Julia McWilliams. She was stationed with the OSS in Ceylon where she administered the OSS Registry overseeing dispatches of the guerrilla warfare against the Japanese. Julia and Paul were romantically involved and she had jumped on a flight to India that day just to spend the evening with him.

The guys prepared the dinner in one of the tent kitchens in the main OSS Detachment 101 training base and served with the whole works on a table in an outside area under netting and with lighted candles and gin and tonic drinks they had pilfered from their British colleagues. The dinner was a huge success as can be seen from this photo of Paul and Julia.

Most will remember her by her married name
"Julia Child"
A name she assumed when she married Paul Child after
the War and made famous on her cooking programs and writings.

And, just maybe, it all started when she fainted after tasting
that magnificent Imam Baldi in Calcutta that Paul and
"Dan" prepared for her.

122

"I was thinking…..Vignettes of a Life Well Spent"

IN SILENT WITNESS

On May 10, 2001 the sculpture "In Silent Witness" by William P. Haas was dedicated at the Newport Public Library, Newport, R.I. with these comments by the donor, Greg Parkos:

The Parkos family is honored to support the work of this distinguished man, Bill Haas, a modern day Renaissance man who is recognized around the world as a scholar of philosophy and history; well known as an academic leader having achieved the Presidency of Providence College and other institutions of higher learning; and a staunch defender of human rights in his role as one of our most prominent teachers of ethics. But underlying all of these achievements is strength and beauty that is the foundation upon which he reflects his love of humanity….He is an artist! Bill Haas may be the man that the great Greek poet Homer wrote about in the Odyssey when he said "This the Gods have wrought; to spin the thread of life 'strong' for some; so that others in time to come may hear their song". This sculpture is his "song" and generations to come will "hear" it.

123

And, the Parkos family recognizes the work of this wonderful institution, The Newport Public Library, which has been a source of inspiration and comfort for the people of this community. No man can ever measure how many great things have been accomplished in this world as a result of the ideas first glimpsed here. Some years ago I was researching the history of the American OSS forces in Burma behind the Japanese lines during World War II and was privileged to secure an interview with one of the key commanders on that mission. After many hours of details about the War and the Kachin tribesmen that they led we sat back, relaxed and talked a little about his personal life.

He had been a television and media correspondent in war and peace for CBS and for Time-Life magazines and was an acknowledge expert on Middle East battles as well as the Vietnam war and he was a prize winning author of a number of books.

His achievements were many so I asked him how and why he had undertaken to pursue such an adventurous life. He responded that beginning when he was about 8 or 9 years old, he started visiting the Newport Public Library which was just around the corner from the little street where he lived and that the librarian started setting aside for him every Friday 3 books for him to take home and read over the weekend. This opened avenues for him to explore in many different worlds and inspired him to achieve a career of significance. That is what the Newport Public Library has done many times.

Lastly, we of the Parkos family recognize the beautiful community of Newport, R. I. It was about 70 years ago during the depth of the Depression that an immigrant couple, refugees from the Balkan Wars, brought their young sons to Newport searching for a better life for their family. The Parkos family found Love, Respect and Opportunity here as well as 3 sisters who were born in Newport and gave us some claim to being Newporters. All 5  children of Teddy and Mary Parkos are here today to say "Thank You Newport"…we are each one of us proud to call this "our home town".

INJUN MARY AND THE FISH BONE LADY

It was about 1936, when I was 6 years old that I first saw her. Intriguing, an American Indian woman in real life and not the movies.

Mary was a large woman, maybe 5ft 9 and weighing about 200 lbs but she was certainly a pretty lady and her manner was soft and gentle with a beautiful soft brown skin tone.

She was my Mother's friend and would visit from time to time to spend the time of day. How these two women became friends was a bit of a mystery because their day to day lives were so different. Mary, the Indian, lived in the same house as we did at 13 Poplar Street but she was outgoing and friendly with everyone and spent almost every evening in the local taverns with her gentlemen friends. Mary, my Mother, stayed at home with her two sons and was too shy to speak to anyone when she was out in the neighborhood. Injun Mary was vibrant and talkative whereas Mom was retiring and silent, perhaps to some extent because her English skills were limited. I don't know how it happened, it just did! Perhaps, in some ways they were both outcasts and that was their common bond.

Injun Mary was less than others and I already knew it despite my early years. When I saw her with men, they were quite a bit less than she deserved. She was sweet and pretty and they were worn out and drunk. It didn't take me long to figure out that in society at that time, she was not considered equal to a comparable quality man just because she was a brown skinned Indian. She had to settle for less.

125

My Mother, the immigrant girl, was also less because she was not an "American" and since she felt that, it became truth. It would take years for her to accept equal status but she did so as her children grew and the family became part of the community. Injun Mary did not have that opportunity since there was no way that her skin could become lighter and her ethnic characteristics would not go away.

On the other hand, there was the fish-bone lady.

This lady was a WASP, an American, the right kind of person for the times in which we lived. I never knew her given name because my Mother always called her Mrs. King and she used to visit as often as Injun Mary but never at the same time.

Mrs. King lived alone near the elementary school that I attended, the Potter School on Elm Street, and she had a Greek immigrant as her lover. George Gavrilos was his name and he never appeared in public with the American lady but it was not difficult to see him going and coming from her home in the evening rather frequently as it was in the neighborhood where we played and lived.

I was frightened by Mrs. King when she visited my Mother because often she was not steady on her feet and she smelled of liquor like you sometimes smelled oozing out of the front doors of the taverns. She was sloppy and disheveled and moved erratically when she walked. I could sense that my Mother did not like her but she was afraid to offend her because of her superior station. It seemed to me that Mrs. King would come to see my Mother especially during those times that she was having a difficult time with her Greek lover and was looking for comfort and understanding.

On one of Mrs. King's visits, she was eating some fish which my Mother had prepared and I remember seeing the fish bones sticking out as she contorted her mouth to speak in her drunken stupor. It frightened me. My Mother tolerated her presence and somehow I was aware that we were treated as lesser people …
…we weren't very much different than Injun Mary!

"I was thinking…..Vignettes of a Life Well Spent"

IS THAT YOU, BLANCHE?

Is it my malleable nature or a heightened sense of introspection that causes me to see myself in so many dramatic characters?

Today, March 26, 2001 is Tom's 90th birthday but Tennessee Williams will not be with us so I am indulging myself with an alone birthday celebration and just thinking about the one character I love most…Blanche. Delusion, desperation, desire, debasement, deranged, what is the word for Blanche to represent me in some part. Is "fantasy" not a gentler word?

As long ago as I can remember, I dreamed of things that were not real but were the hidden drivers within my soul. An actor on the inside portrayed by an actor on the outside and all the while my mind shifting from fact to fiction to embolden my life. No lies on the outside, just interior hope that escalated to the level of dreams and fantasy.

"I have always depended on the kindness of strangers" echoed in my head as I departed from each of my performances in life.

The world was too cruel to play it straight so I used the soft lights and gentle manner of that dream-like trance to win my place whether real or imagined it made no difference. Always I seemed to fool the others, and even sometimes I fooled myself, but not often. I never felt as if I truly deserved whatever goal I had achieved. The trick I thought was to work twice as hard to make up for my inborn inadequacies. It worked outside but not inside.

Once someone asked Tennessee Williams what happened to Blanche after the final curtain and he thought for a moment with his eyes closed and then replied "She will enjoy her time in the bin. She will seduce one or two of the more comely young doctors. Then she will be let free to open an attractive boutique in the French Quarter…."

"She wins?" they asked. "Oh Yes," Williams assured, "Blanche wins."

Thanks, Tennessee Williams, I needed that! And "Happy Birthday."

127

"I was thinking…..Vignettes of a Life Well Spent"

JACLYN, THE DISH WASHER GIRL

In 3 days, it will be the 101st anniversary of my Father's birth and both of my parents have been very much on my mind these days as I approach my own 69th birthday next month. Today I heard a story that relates to them.

There is only one Grandchild that my Mother never knew and that is my daughter, Jaclyn. I am sure that she would have adored our Jaclyn and would be honored that I call her "Jaclyn, the Dishwasher Girl" for this story.

Jaclyn is on a work program in connection with her special education training at Barrington High School and her job every week is to go to a little restaurant in Barrington, Rhode Island, called "The Kozy Kitchen" where she washes dishes and she is paid a nominal amount by the owner for those services. The experience of doing a job and earning compensation is important to the development and self-esteem of children like Jaclyn.

Today, when she had finished her duties at The Cozy Kitchen, the owner gave her an envelope with $50.00 in it and said "Jackie, I want you to take this money and have some fun with it in California on St Valentine's Day as my gift when you go to visit your Daddy next week."

Then he went on to say "Won't you please remember to send me a postcard, I would really like to receive one from California." I do not know this man at all but I am so indebted to him for treating my daughter in such a special way that he will be in my prayers. And, of course, Jaclyn and I will send him a postcard every day of Jaclyn's week here in California.

Just as my Mother introduced herself as "Mary, the Salad Girl" with pride and a measure of her own worth as a person and worker, so too does my Jaclyn wear her special designation "Jaclyn, the Dishwasher Girl" with pride and a measure of her own worth. There is dignity in those titles as they suggest honest and prideful work without pretense.

I guess I am reminded again that: *"No man stands as tall as when he stoops to help a person with special needs."*

128

"I was thinking…..Vignettes of a Life Well Spent"

JOBLESS!

I lost my job today. Mark it well, August 7, 2007, while in my 78th year, I was asked to resign as a Director of Alga Plastics Company and I am unemployed for the first time in the last 69 years.

When did it begin? I remember bits and pieces of that very terrible time of The Great Hurricane and Tidal Wave that smashed into Newport, Rhode Island, on September 21, 1938. The aftermath left all the downtown stores with several feet of water and silt…a very big clean-up job that would take many days before they could conduct normal business again. Mrs. Katherine Jenkins, who ran the boutique "Ann's Hat Shop" on Thames Street named after her mother, was desperately searching for someone to clean up the shop.

My Dad, who was very well known in our town at this time because of his heroic rescue of a number of families from the wharves of Newport as the tide was rising, suggested to her that his 8 year old son, Gregory, was now old enough to work. So, I got my first job in life at Ann's Hat Shop.

We swept and cleaned and mopped for several days before the shop was ready to open again and Mrs. Jenkins handed me three dollars for my efforts together with an offer of continued employment. For the next two years, I went to her store every Monday after school to sweep the floor and make up hat boxes and whatever else she wanted me to do for which she paid me one dollar each week.

129

In 1940, I became an entrepreneur at the age of 10 and started my own business with my brother, John. We built shoe shine boxes and hit the streets of Newport, and the bars, offering to polish the shoes of our clients who mostly were sailors at the Newport Naval Training Station being prepared for war and who got a chance to spend a few hours in town on the weekends. We asked for a nickel and almost always got a dime for what may have been the worst shoeshine imaginable. The barkeeps and the owner of the local strip=tease joint would kick us out whenever they caught us in the bar polishing shoes for some sailor.

At 11 years of age, in 1941, I got a payroll job earning $6 per week (from which 6 cents was deducted for social security) as a shoe shine boy at the City Hall Shoe Repair shop on Broadway. Our specialty was the electric brush shoe shine. The shine cost 10 cents and most customers gave us a 5 cent tip even if we did stain their white socks with shoe polish.

The following year, the owner of that business gave me a job at his cleaning factory "The Valet" earning Fourteen dollars per week...I was on my way up. And then in 1943, at thirteen, I left that job to work with my father at the Puritan Lunch as a dishwasher for zero pay but in the interest of the family business. When my Dad opened the Supreme Lunch a year later, I became a counter man and later a short order cook, but the pay was only my allowance. I loved every minute of it.

And then after my education, the Army and the Foreign Service and Academia and a long list of Corporate positions which ended today when I lost my job and now.....I am jobless!

The day is ending and it's time for me to gather myself and get ready for the pursuit of my next occupation for it's too early for me to quit. Can I sing a song for you? How about.....
"Thanks for the Memories."

"I was thinking…..Vignettes of a Life Well Spent"

KYRIA ELENI & THE ANDARTE
(Lady Helen & The Guerillas)

During my foreign tour of service in the early 1950's, one of the finest Gendarmerie officers I met was a Captain Mallios, Chief of Police in Mytilini, capital city of the Island of Lesbos in Greece. For his police work, he was widely respected throughout the country. Most important, he was a great friend and colleague of mine.

During one of my trips in 1954, Captain Mallios suggested we visit a remote corner of Lesbos where he wanted to introduce me to a heroine of the Greek Civil War which was fought essentially from the end of 1944, when the German occupation forces were expelled from Greece by the British, until 1949, when the Communist revolutionaries were finally expelled into the Iron Curtain countries.

Her name was Kyria Eleni and she was an expatriate from Turkey and part of the population exchange of 1923 under the Treaty of Lausanne. Mallios thought it would be a mutually rewarding visit since he remembered that my own family were Greeks from Turkey and that Kyria Eleni was staunchly anti-communist and a friend of the United States of America, which I represented.

With Captain Mallios and my aide, George Triantafillides, we drove up the primitive roadway system to pay our respects to Kyria Eleni. Along the way, after stopping by the roadside to pick some ripe figs and some fresh oranges growing in the wild as a token gift for this lady patriot, we approached the gateway to her home. A demure lady with a broadly smiling face came out of the house to meet us with her arms outstretched to embrace Captain Mallios.

They were both heroes of the campaign to prevent the takeover of Greece by the Communist military unit E.L.A.S. often referred to as "Andarte", which translated from Greek means "Rebel." Kyria Eleni extended the same warm greeting to all of us and welcomed us into her home.

131

Since she already knew about the origins of my family, she invited us to partake of a classic Greco-Turkish meal on the large porch type veranda overlooking the valley below her home. The special food she had prepared was called "Pastroma" a strongly garlic laced spiced beef dish which would require a steel lined stomach unless you were raised on this kind of food.

It was a daunting experience to please this lady who had gone to some great effort to make a special plate and still deal with my unsympathetic stomach which was agonizing.

 While sipping on a glass of Retsina wine and eating around the edges of my plate of Pastroma, I asked Kyria Eleni if she would tell me the story of her exploits during the civil war. Of course, she insisted they were not really very important but she did remember one event which she thought I might find amusing. It seems there were Andartes in the area who had been ravaging the countryside exploiting their armed presence to pillage from the innocent people whenever they saw something they wanted.

When a band of about a half-dozen rebels approached Kyria Eleni's house, she invited them to come and share some food with her and she gave them wine to drink while she cooked.

Sitting on the veranda they were quite relaxed and when the food was ready, Kyria Eleni spread the meal out on a table before them and then quietly slipped away.

As they were drinking and eating, Kyria Eleni went to an area under the house which normally housed the sheep during the nights and located some dynamite which she had hidden there for use in her war efforts. She quietly set up a major explosive device under the veranda and left the house in the opposite direction of the dining partisans . When she reached the fields behind the house, she lit the fuse that she was carrying with her and fell to the ground to await the big bang.

In less than 60 seconds, the whole veranda was blown skyward with all the participants flying into the sky in bits and pieces.

When she finished the story, I took her hand and asked her to please sit near me while I finished my meal as I did not want her out of my sight while dining and drinking on her veranda.

As the laughter ended, we stepped outside for this photograph:

What a day! What a lady! What a story! What a life!

"   I was thinking.....Vignettes of a Life Well Spent"

MARBLES

I was 9 years old or so and therefore it must have been 1939 in the quiet City of Newport on the Island of Aquidneck in the State of Rhode Island and the Providence Plantations.

An interesting aside that almost noone knows...how did the State of Rhode Island get its name? It just so happens that a British Captain sailing off Narragansett Bay in the Atlantic looked upon Aquidneck Island and thought that it reminded him of the Island of Rhodes in the Mediterranean.

Now, back to our adventurous young boy of 9 on the streets of Newport. It was not unusual for the youngsters of the city to walk in and out of the three "Five and Ten Cent Stores" located on Thames Street after school and on Saturday afternoons. Newport was very much a walking city and that section of Thames Street housed most of the retail stores that catered to the ordinary folks of the town. These three stores were Fishman's, Newberry's and the biggest of them all, the Woolworth store, my favorite.

I had cased the Woolworth store many times looking at the fabulous items on display right there on the counter open for all the world to see. Separated by glass partitions was row upon row of novelties and toys for the delight of all youngsters. There were spinning tops, toy soldiers, games, prizes, and all kinds of glistening and marbleized glass balls called "marbles."

How I loved the sparkle and heft of those agates. I had developed a scheme for gently and silently lifting a few of them off of the counter by laying my right hand flat on top of the marbles and then slowly dipping my third and fourth finger into the stock of marbles just enough to grasp two or three of the marbles into my palm where I would hold them until I left the store. The counter was only six or seven feet from the large double door that led to the Street.

No sooner had I accomplished this magnificent caper, then I felt the large firm hand of the store manager on my right shoulder...I was traumatized! "Let's see what you have there, young man" were the chilling sounds from his mouth that meant I was in big trouble.

The manager knew who I was and that my family lived about four or five blocks away on the same Thames Street. That was not unusual in a small town like Newport. He walked me home to where my Mother was hanging clothes to dry on the clothes' line in the backyard of the "two-tenement" house where we rented the upstairs unit. He addressed my Mother with respect and showed her the evidence of my theft....the tears that filled her eyes and the lament in her voice when she said to me "You have disgraced our family" were the severest punishment I could have been given that day.

My Grandfather, who was semi retired and lived with us in the spare room in the attic, came home later that afternoon. When he heard about my misadventures he slapped me across the buttocks and scolded me for causing such despair to my Mother. When my Father returned home in the evening, his anger was even greater and could only be satisfied by teaching me with his shaving strap across my behind that we were a family of honor and that I had disgraced our entire family by stealing.

The strapping and slapping hurt a little bit but the tears and lament of my Mother stayed with me the rest of my life to remind me that I was dearly loved and that I had a sacred responsibility to my family to reflect in every way the goodness they represented.

I thank God for that store manager who cared enough to do the right thing.

"I was thinking…..Vignettes of a Life Well Spent"

Mary . Mary , quite contrary,

How does your garden grow?

With silver bells and cockle shells,
And pretty maids all in a row.

On February 17, 1956 during a quiet Thursday afternoon Mary, resting at the rear of the Stardust Lounge and lamenting the loss of her brother just 31 days earlier, watched with disbelief as her husband slumped at the front of the store where he had been looking out on Broadway. When she reached him, Teddy was dead of a heart attack. In that instant at age 47, Mary became a widow of modest means with three daughters at home…Estelle, a 19 year old college student; Barbara, a 16 year old high school student; Elaine, a 10 year old elementary school student…and two sons…Greg, a 25 year old with the government abroad; John, a 24 year old Korean War veteran. Mary never flinched, not then, not ever. She worked at whatever job she could get…personal cook, salad girl, whatever was available she did to take care of the girls and she raised them with great success.

Her reward? She lived another 23 years and rejoiced in seeing each one of her children bring to her a grandchild to honor their parents….Barbara brought Pamela (Panagiota) named for Mary; John brought Kerry (Theodosios) named for Teddy; Elaine brought Maria (Panagiota) named for Mary; Estelle brought Mary Vanessa (Panagiota) named for Mary; and Greg brought January (Panagiota) named for Mary and Jaclyn (Theodosia) named for Teddy.

Mary's garden grows very well indeed with six grandchildren named in honor of Mary and Teddy…so long as any of us remembers Mary and Teddy and their names, they continue to live with us all.

136

"I was thinking…..Vignettes of a Life Well Spent"

MATTAPAN

I only made the trip once and then I must have been about 7 years old. The scene is in my mind clearly still. Although there were others there that day I can only remember 3 that I knew. Who took us there and how is completely lost to me except that I do not remember that it was anyone in my family.

It was a big cemetery named Mount Hope and it was stuck right alongside the main heavy traffic business street of the dingiest city I had ever seen, Mattapan, outside Boston. Along that thoroughfare was store after store selling everything imaginable and many of them using the Hebrew letters of the Jews in their signs. There were shoe stores, grocery stores, delicatessens, clothing shops, just about anything you can imagine and none of the stores were very big and each of the stores were family businesses where you could see different members of the family coming and going just within the shops. It was a fascinating neighborhood to this little boy but awfully frightening at the same time.

The trolley cars were rolling along the tracks in the middle of street with their brakes screeching every couple of minutes. People getting off and others getting on. It looked like humanity was going every which way on that boulevard of excitement…

…but not here in the cemetery. My mother was carefully trimming the grass and weeds that had accumulated on top of the graves of her mother and grandmother.

She even sang a little as she did that and seemed to be talking both to me and to them as she went about her effort. There was not much to do…the graves were the simplest possible…just two places in the weeds with the grave marker pronouncing to the world that here two women were buried.

My maternal grandmother and her mother in law were both struck down within days of each other in the Black Plague of 1918 almost twenty years ago.

As my mother told me that story while we busied ourselves cutting large weeds, I was having trouble understanding that here was my mother still a young woman at 28 years old and she had not had a mother since she was 10 years old, not much older than me. And also lost her grandmother right after that.

It was really fascinating how she talked and sang to me and to her mother and grandmother at the same time during our entire visit there. She came to pay her respects but she also came to fill a terrible big void in her heart. As I reflect upon it now…she saw in her children as they came to her over the years one by one, a little bit more erasure of the insidious nickname that the Greek women has given her as a young girl, "To Orphano" (the orphan) and the slow but gradual and sure filling of that void of being without family.

About forty feet away in the cemetery was a man who he intrigued me because my mother called him Theo Gregori (Uncle Gregory)…but Gregori was also what she called me so I was really interested in this older man carrying my name around as if he owned it.

He was very interesting in his manner and style. A really good looking man although short in stature and he choose to talk to my mother and to me in Greek but it did not bother him that I responded mostly in English. Although he was not technically my mother's Uncle, he had been married to Caliope Bartis whose sister, Irene, actually raised my mother.

And now, Theo Gregori was visiting the grave of his great love. He made a place for himself right alongside her grave marker and opened a bag he had brought with him.

Although I can not remember everything that was in that bag, I do remember a tomato, and a piece of cheese and some bread. He sat down eating his lunch there with his beloved and talking to her about matters affecting the family.

He spoke to her in Greek but I understood the essence of what he was saying. On her grave marker was a sealed photograph of the young woman in her wedding gown and Theo Gregori spoke directly to that photograph.

He kissed the photograph and said "Adieu, Agape Mou" (Goodbye, my love) just as down the path, my mother with tears flowing down her face was singing "Ah Manoula Mou" (Oh, dear mother).

And then we left…a little more fulfilled on the inside.

"I was thinking.....Vignettes of a Life Well Spent"

MEMORIES OF OLD LOVES

When I sit and reflect upon my life, the seasons change like a moveable feast.

At each point in my life, the four seasons of life; Spring, Summer, Fall, and Winter; shifted to new dimensions. When I was 40, the summer was my 20's and 30's., and when I was 60, the summer had become my 30's, 40's, and 50's.

The summer keeps getting longer to suit my time span and the winter comes later.

Now as I try to remember that long summer before my most current winter, I have difficulty remembering the individual kisses of earlier loved ones, the warmth of comfort of their individual embraces, and I recognize that all those loves have come and gone because I am now at the end as I feel it currently...and I can't detail them.

I only know that I have loved and that those earlier loves have left me without many specific individual memories but with a warm glow signifying that I have been loved a lot and, in return, I loved a lot.

So, if you were on the list I thank you very much.

But, if you were not on the list I am sorry I missed loving you.

Love is a many-splendored thing!

"I was thinking.....Vignettes of a Life Well Spent"

MOM! I'M HOME!

As my teacher, Miss. Martin, of the third grade dismissed us from Potter School that afternoon in 1939, I bolted out the door and headed up Potter Street turning right on Cross Street and then dashing down the few blocks to 82 Thames Street where we lived in a rented second-floor tenement. I bolted up the outdoor front stairs through the front double door and up the inside staircase to the landing where the door to our tenement was always open.

Bursting through the front door, I announced loudly "Mom! I'm Home!" The silence was deafening to my ears as the stillness of our tenement struck me with concern....nobody was there. Searching the rooms and the attic upstairs as well as glancing out the windows onto the back year convinced me that our home was empty of family. Mom had always been there before except for the time when my little sister, Estelle, was born so I had always assumed she would always be there when I got home from school.

This day was different. Maybe she took the baby to the Doctor, maybe she was with relatives on a special mission, maybe she was at church, or maybe she was out shopping. Convincing myself that there was nothing to worry about, I then took the same exact next steps that I always followed when arriving home from school. Entering the kitchen, I pulled open the Ice Box to view the contents.

The third shelf from the bottom which normally contained the glasses of Greek Yoghurt that Mom would make weekly seemed rather empty and only one little glass was in place on the wire rack. It was a puny looking sample of her marvelous Yoghurt but that was all that was there so it would have to do.

Searching for a piece of bread in the cabinet I was lucky enough to find a thick slice of yesterday's Vienna loaf. It was the same thing I ate every afternoon when I returned from school...a glass of Yoghurt and a slice of crusty bread.

Within seconds with the help of a trusty spoon I had devoured both the Yogurt and the hefty bread. It tasted so good that now I was ready to go outside and play games with my friends of the neighborhood.

When I returned home later that afternoon, my Mother was waiting for me with an unpleasant look on her face and admonished me:"You ate my Magia, the Yogurt culture that I use as a starter. "

Without that culture there would be no more Yogurt in our home and thus began the relentless search for a substitute culture to use in this horrible situation. It was then that it dawned on me that the stuff that was in a smaller glass in the Ice Book was not the regular Yogurt but was in fact the culture that was the breeding start of each new batch of this wonderful food and without which, no new Yogurt could be made. It was not sold in stores, it was something that families handed down from generation to generation and now our family treasure had been consumed for a momentary satisfaction.

Searching among the ladies of the Greek Orthodox Church in Newport, Mom found the best source for a sample culture that might be similar to her own and that was with Venetia Bartis. Venetia was the wife of John Bartis whose sister, Irene, had married my Mother's Uncle and helped raised my Mother and her siblings when their Mother and Grandmother died while they were still very young children. All of that relationship stuff would make Venetia's culture a substitute for the treasure that I had destroyed in my gluttony.

We trekked up to Tilden Avenue to the Bartis second floor tenement where a very small sample of Venetia's culture was transferred to my Mom and then we dashed home to make a batch of Yogurt with the hope that it would take hold and produce an acceptable product for us.

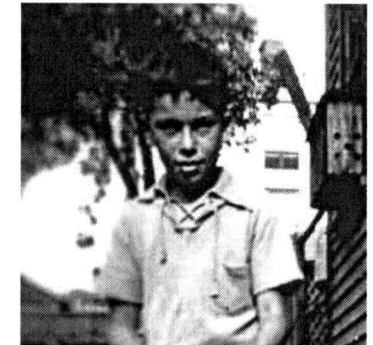

It worked! And I was forgiven my transgressions.

"I was thinking.....Vignettes of a Life Well Spent"

MOM'S WISH

Mom would have been 89 years old just a few days ago...July 5, 1997...and she was on my mind all week. Funny how the days all came together and reached a crescendo bursting aloud in my mind on Sunday the 6th of July 1997. We celebrated the Sunday of the Saint Kiriaki on that day and also celebrated the one year anniversary of the baptism of my Nadine (actually on June 30th....she was named Kyriaki by her Godmother, my sister Elaine).

For the first time since Easter week, my mother was not with me in Church and I couldn't figure out what was wrong...why had she abandoned me now? Why is she unhappy with me now? What was different?

I could only conclude that she felt I had taken a turn that she did not like; I had turned away from my responsibility as head of the family and turned inward for a little while. The drain had been too much. Their needs for my presence in their lives too great. I needed a break and I felt my teachings were falling on deaf ears. My work was now more demanding so I had a good excuse to cut out and besides which when I had admonished my nephew, Teddy, to remember his work ethic his mother suggested that perhaps I needed to tend to my own affairs and leave others alone...I was happy to do so.

This is not the first time my Mother has looked away from me. I failed her once before when she died and I was not able to keep her children from bickering about their inheritance. A very sad time. It was my responsibility to my mother to see that there was continuing peace among her children and I failed. It is hurtful to contemplate how even the most loving families can be torn asunder by money. That matter was settled with the traditional silver but now I need a more personal way to get myself back in my Mom's good graces.

143

I read the writings of those who remember her gracious and funny ways and who reflect upon how they loved and do miss her and it reminds me of a biblical line...."Were you there when they nailed my Jesus to the Cross?" Some were there but most were not.

Mom was funny and she was sentimental but she was more...she would not have left someone hanging on a Cross.

The last time I saw my Mother was on my birthday in 1978 just a few days before she died practically in my sister Elaine's arms. I wish I had been with her at that last moment. She blessed my daughter January on the last day I spent with her by calling her "Sunday", which in Greek is Kiriaki. Elaine chose that name for Nadine to continue my Mother's presence in my life.

Were you there when my Mother died? No, I don't mean physically, I mean spiritually. Were you there when they nailed my Jesus to the Cross?

I end now. Nothing more to say. Perhaps reflection will bring me back to the role my Mom intends for me. If it means she will come back to be with me in Church, I will do it at once.

Let's see what she says this Sunday.

"I was thinking…..Vignettes of a Life Well Spent"

MOTHER'S LAMENT

Her voice was soft on the telephone and it trembled as she said "Greg, Cousin Danny has died!" I gasped, caught my breath and slumped in my chair….it was my mother's voice.

It was February 15, 1965 and Damon A. Diomandes had just turned 43 years old less than two months before. To Mom he was more than a cousin since his mother, Aunt Irene, had raised them together with their siblings as one family because my mother and her siblings became like orphans when their mother and grandmother died in the 1918 Plague. When Danny arrived as the first born in 1922, my mother and her siblings were already in his mother's care. My maternal grandfather and Danny's father were brothers.

Monday was never a very good day but this particular Monday took on an especially bad feeling since Danny had been one of my personal special heroes.

 I was only 11 years old when he went off to war immediately after Pearl Harbor and I remember clearly his innocent but patriotic look. He followed in the footsteps of his father, a new immigrant in the time of the Great War who volunteered to serve for his new country and become an American citizen just as my own father had. Danny was 19 years old when he enlisted.

Danny's outfit landed in NorthAfrica in November of 1942 together with the British to fight the the Axis in Casablanca, Oran, Algiers, Tunis, Bizerte and Libya until the Germans surrendered in June of 1943 followed in September 1943 by the invasion of Sicily. In the battle for Monte Casino, Danny received his first wound of the war, despite his markings indicating that he was a medic, while he was giving aid to a fallen comrade.

After D-Day in 1944, Danny joined the Allied forces in France and Germany until the end of the war serving as medic for one battle after another and took his second wound while once again helping a fallen comrade. He was given the Bronze Star for his heroic deed of saving the lives of his comrades while

under heavy fire. The end of his military service in this war found him at the gates of the infamous death camp called Dachau where he was one of the first Americans to enter the camp and went quickly to the aid of those devastated Jewish prisoners who were emaciated and dying minute by minute even as they were being liberated.

At the end of the War in August of 1945, Danny came marching home to his family in Newport, Rhode Island, and took off his uniform for his work of fighting a war and saving his comrades was done for this 23 year old hero. He wooed and wed a beautiful local girl named Sophie Borodemos and joined her father in his very famous local diner named Tommy's Diner as a partner together with his brother-in-law Demo who had also just returned from the War in

Europe where he had been a Prisoner of War of the Germans.

By January of 1948, Danny and Sophia had their first child named Gary and life was just grand for this young couple as the first born was followed by siblings every couple of years so that by 1965, they had five kids from 17 years old to 4 years old. After Gary, there was Paula, Sandra, Tommy and Dean. The business was good and it looked like a happy time coming up for Damon A. Diomandes.

The end came swiftly and with no warning. Danny was dead and the family gathered in Newport to put him to rest. What three years of enemy fire could not do to this heroic medic who carried no firearms while in the field of battle, came quickly and for no clear reason. But, it happened and that was that so we tend to those who are left behind. Of course, I rushed to my mother's home as soon as I could and prepared to be with her during the wakes and the funeral which we attended together since I was her oldest and she was widowed. The sadness was deep and there was no attempt at light heartedness since the death of such a young man had taken our breath away.

Sitting next to my mother at the second pew on the right side, I was deep in prayer and remembrance when a low level of sound that was like the moaning of a crippled being began as a plaint and slowly increased in volume over the next several minutes to a groan of pain and then unto the wail of the desperate and finally the screech and howl of those who have lost their soul. It was Danny's mother sitting in the first seat of the pew before me at St. Spyridon's Church. I was stunned into breathlessness as I had never heard that kind of pain and I could not breathe.....my mother's right hand clasped my left hand and the sharpness of that pain brought me back to consciousness.

That was the first time I had ever heard a "Mother's Lament." The service ended and we followed the casket to its final resting place and then we gathered to speak our stories of this man.

Danny's mother, whom we all called Aunt Irene, had raised my mother but she had never really felt like a grandmother to me. Can't explain why, but she just never did. But on this night, she took me to her side and holding my hand cried softly in a broken voice:

"There is no greater pain than
a mother's burial of her first born!"

That was just a little more than 42 years ago this night and I have never forgotten that moment. It is burned into my memory forever. I thought at the time that I would never hear that sound of a Mother's Lament dirge ever again, but I was wrong. It happened one more time some years later.

Johnny Giacchi was a very successful entrepreneur who had returned from the service to put a small printing press in the backroom of his father's grocery store in the Italian district of Providence. He started out by printing invitations and business cards for people of Federal Hill and he grew that business into a major manufacturer of printed cards and thermoformed blisters for many consumer products. When he had progressed from the invitations to the point of printing headers for poly bags used at retail stores, we became friends and I helped him establish a cost accounting system for his company so that he could price his wares effectively. Johnny, who was nicknamed "Jay", never forgot that help and he was always a gracious gift giver at every holiday event.

We were fast friends even though we drifted apart as I began my journey into Corporate America and he built a truly innovative and successful company called "Jay Printing Company" which became the dominant supplier in the retail packaging industry.

When I moved to California and was elected President of Whittaker Corporation, a Fortune 500 company, John sent me a telegram which simply said:

"YOU DONE GOOD!"

It was painful to hear a few years later that John Giacchi had died but I had to be there for his funeral as he was my friend. The funeral home was filled and I sat quietly by myself in the last row of seats while the Priest began a lamentation of departure.

Suddenly, it happened again exactly as I had remembered it. A low level of sound that was like the moaning of a crippled being began as a plaint and slowly increased in volume over the next several minutes to a groan of pain and then unto the wail of the desperate and finally the screech and howl of those who have lost their soul. It was John's mother sitting in the first row of seats.

"There is no greater pain than
a mother's burial of her first born!"

"I was thinking…..Vignettes of a Life Well Spent"

MOURNING

The Greeks have a word for it, "DiploAgoni", and Panagiota knew the term very well for she had suffered it not once but twice in her lifetime.

This 4 year old girl arrived in America in the Fall of 1912 with her father, mother and grandmother after burying her baby brother, Ioannis, in the village of Kerassia, Turkey. The earthquake that killed her 1 year old brother had devastated the village. He was crushed by the falling stonewalls of their home. The clouds of war were hovering over the Balkans and, with nature's wrath visited upon them in the form of the earthquake, the father, Stergios, decided to take his family to America to begin a new life.

They settled on Tyler Street in Boston. It was an area where all the new immigrants who arrived in Boston began. And within a year another daughter, Sophia, was born, to be followed within another 2 years in 1915 by a new brother, Damon. The family had been reconstituted as their new life unfolded. By September 1918, Panagiota was already starting in the fifth grade of school, her younger sister Sophie was beginning school and 3 years old Damon was happy at home with his mother, Styliani, and his paternal grandmother, named Smaragda. Life was good for this 10-year-old girl.

Then the first "DiploAgoni" happened. In September 1918, soldiers at an Army base started to die from a strain of Influenza called the Black Plague, the worst epidemic in American history, killing over 600,000. In early October, Panagiota's mother was one of that number and the family was now in the care of the grandmother. By the end of October 1918, the grandmother succumbed to the same death and they were left with a decimated family of a father and 3 young children aged 10, 5, and 3. The "DiploAgoni" had struck before Panagiota had even ended the deep mourning for the loss of her mother. This loss, compounded by the later uprooting of her family to live with an aunt and uncle as "orphans" cast shadowS on her happy heart that stayed with her literally until she had her own family of children...and then one by one as they came, the shadow withdrew and she found happiness with the joy of a family together as one unit with her husband and five children.

150

Blessed are those who mourn for they shall be comforted.

The years went by. Panagiota had to drop out of school to help her aunt with the family chores. She grew into a young lady of grace and was married. Although suffering the economic difficulties of the Thirties, she emerged in the Forties with her own home and family all doing well and happy in Newport, Rhode Island. Not a single human being could even imagine a negative thought about this charitable, gentle and loving woman. Her brother and her first cousin (with whom she was raised as a brother) had gone off to war and returned safely, her sons had served in the military and returned safely. It should have been an era of Ouzo and Baklava.....but that was not to be just yet.

A second "DiploAgoni" catapulted upon Panagiota. Her brother, Damon, the little baby of 1915 who grew to serve in combat behind the enemy lines in World War II leading Kachin tribesmen against the Japanese, died in the hospital in an unexpected way. Damon was more than her younger brother; in many ways he was her son also. When she and her sister and brother moved in with the aunt, of course Panagiota had to be responsible for the care of her own siblings. Even though Sophia was only 5 years younger and Damon was 8 years younger, she was their "in spirit Mommy".

The loss was hard for Panagiota. It contradicted the natural order of things. He was the youngest. Why should he have been called to go before her? And worst, like a replay of a bad movie she had seen this scene before. A parent dying and leaving behind 3 young children. Deja Vu! Deep, deep sadness and maybe more than at any time in their life together, her husband Theodosios held her close and comforted her while he himself agonized over this unnatural early death.

And then, again the second half of the "DiploAgoni" struck. Within 30 days. Panagiota's husband fell as she was watching him at their place of business and died immediately. When she realized what had happened and that Theodosios was dead, her mouth opened to scream but no sound came out for she was gasping with agony.

Blessed are those who mourn for they shall be comforted.

It was time for a different type of healing to take place; it had to be her larger family, her children's families, who would fill the void, and they did. She reveled as each was married and as each brought new children into her family. By the time of her final illness in the late Seventies, Panagiota was a fulfilled woman again and very happy in her life with her family.

Panagiota was my mother, Mary Diomandes Parkos.

Blessed are those who mourn, for they shall be comforted

Photograph by Barbara Parkos at Island Cemetery, Newport, R.I.
April, 2000

152

"I was thinking…..Vignettes of a Life Well Spent"

MY BROTHER JOHN'S WEDDING
Oct 4, 1998

As I listened to the Gospel today I was reminded that just two years ago Nadine and I stood at the place of that wedding in Cana where Jesus performed the first miracle of his ministry just 3 days after the call of the first disciples at the Sea of Galilee

Just 3 days before His crucifixion and the end of his ministry, Jesus is quoted at great length by Matthew in Chapter 25 and the majestic climax of that discourse reminded me of my brother, John.

"for…I was a stranger and you took me in"

On the night that John was being delivered by a cluster of our countrywomen in the first floor tenement of the Stratis family home in Somerville, Massachusetts, I was being held by our Aunt Sophie in the doorway of the bedroom and just as my brother was issued forth from the womb of our Mother, I was taken from her arms by Pagiou, the Matriarch of our village family, and she placed me face to face with this new baby and shouted into my face a single word "Adelphos" (the Greek word for brother) and then immediately turned to the baby and shouted the same word into his face "Adelphos". Neither one of us would ever be a stranger again because we had each other for eternity because we were "Brothers".

"for..I was naked and you clothed me"

Time went by and we started to play the backyard games and get into trouble every once in a while with other kids. John was a lot more aggressive than I was as a youngster so it was natural that the neighborhood bullies would pick on me. As they pushed me in a provoking manner, I would glance to my left and there alongside me was my brother, John, with his hands raised in a menacing way defending me because we were "Brothers".

At night, we shared a single bed in a little unheated room in the front of our tenement in Newport, Rhode Island, and we learned to depend on each other's body heat to keep warm because we were "Brothers".

"for I was hungry and you gave me food"

My brother, John, went off to War and I stayed home to continue my studies but not without his unwavering support both spiritually and financially at times because we were "Brothers".

"for...I was thirsty and you gave me drink"

And later when I had the unique opportunity of a lifetime to invest as a major principal in a new business for the first time, I was short by about half the money I needed and he opened his purse and told me to borrow whatever I was short....there were no papers, no lawyers, no interest, no strings attached,...because we were "Brothers".

"for..I was sick and you visited me"

Perhaps when I needed him most in life on a personal basis was when I was alone in Newport in 1992 and suffering terrible aloneness.
He walked with me and wept with me and finally convinced me to get up off the mat and pursue my dreams which culminated in the great romance of my life with my Nadine...because we were "Brothers".

And...Jesus said
"As you did this to one of the least of these my brethren, you did it to me and you will join the righteous in eternal life".

I toast you John for without you I would not have had the wonderful life I have had... because we were "Brothers".

Kathy, you are a beautiful and loving lady and I give you one of the most precious things in the world to me...My Brother John.

"I was thinking…..Vignettes of a Life Well Spent"

MY DAUGHTER'S WEDDING

As I walked down the aisle with you, January, and listened to Joni Mitchell's The Circle Game, I thought about…

This past decade or so....together....

...We shopped at the Grand Bazaar in Istanbul and we kissed the Blarney Stone in Ireland.

...We danced Flamenco with the Gypsies in Spain and we sang Reggae all night long in Jamaica.

...We climbed the Pyramids in Cairo and we rode the Gondolas along the canals of Venice, Italy.

...We sat on top of the Acropolis in Athens and we even went "Stomping at the Savoy" in London on New Year's Eve to celebrate your 21st birthday....and many other journeys too numerous to count.

Now...Today...our journey ends as you begin a new era in your life with a new companion for the rest of your life.

"Thanks for the Memories....I will miss you...May God be with you all the days of your life."

June 5, 2004

"I was thinking…..Vignettes of a Life Well Spent"

MY FRIEND, EROLLE HAAS

The great historian, Stephen E. Ambrose wrote the following words in his book called "Comrades":

"Friendship is different from all other relationships. Unlike acquaintanceship it is based on love. Unlike lovers and married couples it is free of jealousy. Unlike children and parents it knows neither criticism nor resentment. Friendship has no status in law. Business partnerships are based on a contract. So is marriage. Parents are bound by the law, as are children. But friendship is freely entered into, freely given, freely exercised.

"Friends never cheat each other, or take advantage, or lie. Friends do not spy on one another, yet they have no secrets. Friends glory in each other's successes and are downcast by the failures. Friends minister to each other, nurse each other. Friends give to each other, worry about each other, stand always ready to help.

"Perfect friendship is rarely achieved,
but at its height it is an ecstasy."

With some encouragement, Erolle Haas spoke into his tape recorder some thoughts from his life. I have compiled those comments just as he spoke them with his style and manner of speech untouched. There are some things too sacred to be edited and this work is one of those. This story is for his children, my children and everyone's children. It is an American story. Could not happen anywhere else in this world and reflects the very greatness of this country. Erolle J. Haas lived his life in "The Arena" where his face was marred by dust and sweat and blood and yet he strove valiantly to spend himself in a worthy cause and to know the triumph of high achievement…his "_Continuum._"

156

"I was thinking.....Vignettes of a Life Well Spent"

NAMES

God! It has been hard to explain...again and again...the same story to the same people and nobody remembers its telling....where will the story be when I am gone...lost forever.

The story of a 14 year old boy joining his big brother in a new country thousands of miles away from home and family and as if that were not lonely enough, his big brother, Gregory, left a year later to go and get the rest of the family and he was lost at sea during the tumultuous times that marked the Balkan War of 1913-1914....and the boy was alone.

A proud family from the aristocracy of the dirt....that earth on which the grapes and cherries were plentiful and abounding....and nothing else of value except tradition.

It was the custom of the people in those times to approach names in a very simple and logical way...the first born son would be named to honor his paternal grandfather (but only if the grandfather were not living at the time - these people considered it a death wish to name a child after a living person). The second born son would honor the maternal grandfather with the same caveats. The girls, considered of little importance, had no clear cut pattern for naming but generally they would be named for deceased grandparents or other family members to be honored.

Theodosios was the second born son of Kyriakos and Bourboy and was probably named for his Mother's father but that is just speculation. In the village of Kirassia, the boy was known as "Theodosios, the son of Kyriakos" and all the villagers would know who he was by that method. There were no surnames in the village of Kirassia or in the country of Turkey until 1923 when Kemal Mustafa decreed that everyone must have a surname...and took for himself the name Ataturk, which means "father of the Turks". He had founded the Republic of Turkey which succeeded the Ottoman Empire.

In those very rare cases where someone visited the village who was not intimately aware of all the villagers, a third name would be added to an individual which either described the physical characteristics of the father or his occupation. In that way it was established that this boy's name would be:

THEODOSIOS KYRIAKOS PSIROUKIS

Theodosios was his given name at baptism and Kyriakos was his father's given name. The final name, Psiroukis, refers to a kind of porridge that was a common food in that part of the world. Kyriakos was a brick baker at a brickyard on the shores of the Sea of Marmara just two kiolometers downhill from Kirassia and his favorite daily lunch was a bowl of this particular porridge. Brick baking was this family's occupation in that community. Brick manufacture was the only industry in the area other than fruit and sunflower agriculture.

Now, back to our lonely young man in Boston without his family and thousands of miles from home. As he approached his 19th birthday, the 1st World War was beginniing to heat up and it looked like the United States might become involved. This young man volunteered !

The name had been very difficult for him to figure out in English. When he first arrived, he met another man named Theodosios and asked him "What do the Americans call you?" and that man told him that he was called "George" and then later he met someone named Kyriakos, who said that the Americans called him "Albert". Since he was only accustomed to having two regular names from the old country, that was all he asked for and for a long time he went around and introduced himself to Americans as "George Albert".... a pretty good name for a handsome young man with an eye for the ladies and an inclination toward good times. As time went on, he knew that those name transfers didn't make sense in literal translation but he wasn't sure how to fix them properly.

The Army gave him his chance at the first moment of induction when a grizzly looking Irish-American recruiting Sergeant asked for his name. When the young man said "Theodosios", the tough Sergeant replied "Theodore" because he had no idea what in the world Theodosios meant but it did sound a lot like Theodore. (incidentally Theodosios means "given by God").

When Theodore gave his second name as Kyriakos, the Sergeant was getting a little impatient and just wrote down "K." as a middle initial.

Then the final step..."what's your family name ?" asked the recruiter and Theodore K. answered "Psiroukis" and in the bat of an eye, old grizzly with his eyes rolling up into his head said "Listen Teddy, as a result of serving in combat with the U.S. Army you will automatically become an American, for God's sake, get an American name.".

Now, completely flustered by his new names, Theodore K. (Teddy) thought hard but quickly and the only American name he could think of was the name of the Parker House Hotel where he worked in the kitchen and so he blurted out "Parker".

The Sergeant, now totally exasperated, bellowed out "Don't you know that Greek names end in an 'os' or an 'as' ?"

Then after a moment to calm down, he looked at the new recruit and said:

"O.K., Private Theodore K. Parkos,
you are in the Army now

and

you have a new American name.
Congratulations!"

A footnote....

Teddy Parkos Served with the famed
Second Cavalry Division of the
American Expeditionary Force
during The Great War

and proudly wore many citations
for bravery in battle
together with his comrades and
"Fellow Americans."

"I was thinking…..Vignettes of a Life Well Spent"

"NANETA – A ONE BUCK TRICK"

Often you read authors proclaim they have changed the names of the characters to protect the innocent, this story is very different since the names have been changed to protect the guilty. There are no innocents in this tale.

Zonar's was a famous watering hole at the center of Athens. The tables on the front large boulevard were for those who were comfortable being seen. Around the corner on the side street just behind the Grand Bretagne Hotel is where those not interested in being seen took their places. That is where you would find the "Americans."

The summer of 1954 was grand and the weather was perfect for sipping after work drinks at Zonar's. Work routine during the summer in Athens was early morning from 8 AM, lunch at 1 PM with lots of wine, a nap of an hour or two, return to work at 5 PM, Zonar's for drinks at 8 PM, then dinner at about 10 PM at some taberna, and finally at midnight the Bazooki joints for music and dance

This was the life of these young adventurers during the time they were in Athens at their central offices. Most of the time they were traveling in the remote villages and along the Balkan borders of Greece. Life in the countryside was usually rough. Every couple of weeks the guys would be together again in Athens and that was when they most enjoyed the soft summer evenings.

The "Americans" were a group of young single men who had been sent to Greece by the U. S. Foreign Service during the early 1950s to insure that the agents of the Communist International was not successful in sending their agents to the United States. Many of the Greeks who survived the civil war in their country were sympathetic to the Soviet Comintern and it was a time when many refugees and Iron Curtain escapees were trying to migrate to America.

161

Such a serious business did not preclude a cavalier state of being for these guys however so their time in Athens was often spent in pursuit of the good life despite the seriousness of their mission during other times when they were in the field covering the edges of the Balkans.

Her nickname was Naneta and none knew any more about her. e night she stopped at the table for idle chatter d then spent the night….not with them all but h the one that was most skilled at duction….and his name was Larry.

She was stunningly beautiful with an quisitively curvaceous figure clothed in a nner to insure that every man was able to ualize her nudity. Her chatter was gleeful and manner was flirty. All the guys were aptured with her but Larry became her man. e rest just salivated.

It was a strange relationship since Larry did not know how to contact her but just about every time he was in town and sitting at Zonar's she would walk on by. The strange thing was that when Larry was away the rest of us never saw her.

Larry and Naneta made love madly every couple of weeks or so for over a year and whenever one of those nights happened, Larry's apartment mate had to find someplace else to spend the night. Once in a while, Naneta would bring a friend for Larry's roommate and on those weekends it was always the same routine. Drinking on Saturday night, making love all night and then the men would rise up in the morning, make love one more time and then head out to the American Club in Kifissia for a breakfast of Steak and Eggs with Champagne while the girls stayed behind at the apartment and eventually dressed and went home on their own.

As the year drew to an end, Larry was given orders to leave Athens for another assignment in Europe so his roommate left him with Naneta for a wild weekend of lovemaking before his departure on the Monday morning. His roommate made himself scarce but he was there promptly at 9 AM on that Monday morning to take Larry to the airport. Naneta had already left by then. Larry described the parting as a tearful separation for the two of them.

As Larry packed his clothes and dressed for the trip he suddenly realized that his wallet had been emptied of money. After the shock of the loss wore off and his buddy loaned him enough money for the trip, Larry realized that Naneta had taken $200 from his wallet. To comfort Larry, his friend explained that since she had been with Larry for about 50 evenings during the last year and that since they had made love about 4 times on each of those evenings….by simple arithmetic calculation it had cost Larry only $1 for each time he made love to Naneta.

Alas! The really sad result of this matter was that Naneta was lost to the "Americans" since each of them wanted to take Larry's place.

"I was thinking.....Vignettes of a Life Well Spent"

NO MORE MARTINIS

Before my assignment to Greece in the mid Fifties, I had never been much of a drinker but it was virtually impossible to live there and not consume wine. Lunch and dinner in restaurants was always served with wine and no water, no juice, no soft drinks in all public restaurants for all our meals. My roommate, Bill Crassas, and I never let cooking in our apartment interfere with its "partytime" status.

An then I met this attractive American lady, Georgia Dent Robinson, who was in Greece with her very young daughter, living in a villa style estate just outside of Athens. We started dating a bit so from time to time I would join them at their home for dinner. She had a country girl who prepared meals and took care of their family needs. It wasn't anything serious. I enjoyed her company with no long term interest. This continued for a few months and then...

On a Saturday night while waiting for dinner at the villa she introduced me to a new alcohol drink that I had never tried before called Martini. It was pretty good and she offered me a second one and then a third and maybe a fourth and a fifth and on and on. I woke up the next morning in her bed with a strange feeling of guilt combined with "a fear that I was going to die but afraid that I would not."

When she realized I had awakened, she draped me with her body and cooed to me "I am so happy; my dreams were answered when you asked me to marry you last night and we must start planning for a wedding soon as I want to be your wife and begin our life together."

What was I to do? What can one do? I was stunned into silence and spent many years in atonement. Take this advice from this poor soul if ever you are offered a second martini....simply say:

"No Thanks."

164

"I was thinking…..Vignettes of a Life Well Spent"

NO MORE SUNFLOWERS!

*"No matter what it is you decide to do with your life, be sure
that if asked to write an autobiography, you would be able to
write a historical novel and not a one page essay."*

The Sunflower Fields of Thrace

As you cross these fields of Sunflowers approaching the Sea of Marmara down there to the rear left where the trees are standing, you will find the village of Kerassia in Turkey. A 14 year old boy, Teddy Parkos, left that village in 1912 never to return again as he began an epic odyssey of life.

This is the story of one of the events that made his life so significant.

As soon as he arrived in America in 1912, Teddy got a job at the Parker House in Boston working in the kitchen as a dishwasher. Within a year he had progressed from that job to helping the bakers make Parker House Rolls and preparing Baked Scrod with the cooks. At just about that time in 1913, his older brother, Gregory, who had brought him to this country left to visit the family in Turkey to arrange for their transport to America….and he was never heard from again. The speculation was that either he became ill and died at sea or he became embroiled in the Balkan War which was raging at that time threatening the very existence of all the Greeks in Turkey. Now, Teddy was alone and because of the Balkan War all communications with his family in Turkey ceased.

He worked hard and continued to progress at the Parker House.

During those early years working at the Parker House Teddy was fascinated by the preening manner of Colonel Samuel Parker, the Grandson of the founder of the hotel who had gone to Hawaii many years earlier, married a Princess of the Hawaiian royal family, and became known as "King" of Hawaii. During his visits to Boston Colonel Parker was a familiar sight strolling around Park Square near the Parker House.

Gosh, how much Teddy liked working at the Parker House. He worked there with a couple of his friends, Stratigakis Cazacou and Diamantis Flamouri, from the village of Kerrasia who came to America with him on board the steamship Macedonia to join their brothers arriving on August 12, 1912 at Ellis Island. The Parker House was filled with lots of immigrants from many different countries but his eye went quickly to the young maids of the hotel who were principally from Ireland.

From time to time his boyhood friends would find Teddy teasing one of the Irish girls in the corridor behind the kitchen and before long it looked like he had struck up a romantic association with a pretty lass named "Colleen O'Shea" with bright red cheeks, pale ivory skin, and a lovely curved body that swayed as she walked down the hallways. It was kind of his first girlfriend ever and he kept that relationship private.

Teddy volunteered for the U. S. Army in 1917 when he was just 19 years old and because of his work experience in the kitchen of the Parker House hotel in Boston he was sent to Fort Riley, Kansas, to train at the Cook and Baker's School. That was not what he wanted as he enlisted to fight in the Great War against the Germans who were allied with the Turkish Government who oppressed his family severely during these days.

Teddy was determined not to give up until he could serve in combat against the enemies of his new country. Every day after class instruction Teddy would walk into the Company Headquarters and plead for an assignment to a combat unit. Captain Dan Reynolds, the Company Commander, liked Teddy's spunk especially when he would proclaim "I want to fight" with a slight Greek accent. And Captain Reynolds' response was always "We'll see, Private, we'll see!"

As classes ended on the last day of instruction, Teddy rushed to find the First Sergeant at Company Headquarters to learn about his assignment. "What's for me, Sarge?" he shouted. The seasoned First Sergeant, George Anderson, replied "You got your wish, Teddy, you will be joining the 2nd Cavalry Regiment at Fort Ethan Allen in Vermont. They leave for France in 90 days. Do you know how to ride a horse?"

Teddy was ecstatic. The 2nd Calvary Regiment was the longest continuously serving unit in the United States Army originally established by President Andrew Jackson on May 23, 1836. Off he went to Vermont for training in preparation for combat.

Outfitted in the uniform used by Cavalrymen, Teddy knew how to swagger with his new comrades....and his new black Argentinean horse.

About a month after his arrival a letter was delivered to him at mail call...it was the first letter he was to receive at this station so he was excited to open it. Having forgotten that he had written his old buddies at the Parker House about his new assignment, he was astonished to learn that the letter was from Colleen. He stretched out on the lawn to read it over and over again.

It was a loving note filled with admiration and concern for him and his well-being. After reflecting on the contents overnight, Teddy asked for a weekend pass so that he could visit his "friends' in Boston.

Since they were soon to depart for war, the pass was issued and that next weekend Teddy was on the train to Boston.

Arriving at the South Station in Boston in the early evening Teddy dashed on foot to the Boarding House at Broadway and Stuart where the young Irish girls who worked at the Parker House lived.

When he arrived at the house a number of the girls were sitting in the parlor listening to the radio and they all smiled to see him so resplendent in his dress uniform.

Someone called out in a loud voice "It's Teddy."

A stunned Colleen was laughing and crying when she embraced Teddy.

The rest of the details of that weekend are lost in history but we do know that Teddy was back at his post for Reveille on Monday morning reporting for duty.

What might have happened is best attended to by your imagination. Maybe a walk in the Boston Commons and a visit to Church on Sunday…or maybe something else.

Teddy and the 2nd Cavalry Regiment embarked for Europe soon after that visit and never was he to see Colleen ever again. He went off to War as just a little more than a boy and returned after the Armistice as a whole lot more than just a man.

Clearly material for a "Historical Novel and not a One Page Essay."

Teddy's heroic exploits with the 2nd Cavalry Regiment in France under General "Blackjack" Pershing is another much larger story which we will explore at another time.

ODETTA TONIGHT

Damn, it was hot and humid in Newport…but that is July's curse in that town….and Greg was mad and miserable. No place to go. Certainly not home where she was slushing around in an alcoholic stupor. Nor to Mom's house out of shame for the mess he was in.

Leaving his car in the old Point section of town, he walked along Thames Street with his head dropped down onto his chest in disgust with himself. As darkness settled in, some relief from the heat was felt and Greg lifted his head to the left where a dingy little bar named "The Helm" had a sign in the window announcing "Odetta Tonight."

Oh, what the hell he thought and as he entered the door he mounted a stool right in the middle of a small bar where a half dozen guys were hanging around drinking and laughing. The bartender pulled him down a draft of Bud and Greg just looked into the glass forlornly trying to figure out what the hell to do.

Slowly he felt a nudging to the right as a large body slid into the stool next to him. That was ok with Greg…no problem sharing space. It was 5 or 7 minutes before he realized that his stoolside companion was Odetta! As every fan of Folk and Gospel knew, Odetta was a Queen of that style of singing. Sure the bad times had settled upon her and she had to take a few hundred buck gigs just to survive but she still was a legend to Greg and a multitude of others.

They drank beer and laughed together for another hour before she stepped upon a small stage behind the bar with her guitar to belt out more than an hour of her ballads….she was fantastic! Greg could not wait for her to return to the barstool next to him….but she never did…and he walked out the door alone again.

169

"""I was thinking…..Vignettes of a Life Well Spent"

ON THE ORIENT EXPRESS

It was July of 1955, and Angelo Kalaris was getting a little restless in Athens. One night as he and his closest comrades, Bill Crassas and Greg Parkos, were hanging out at a Bazookie joint in Athens, he blurted out "Let's get out of this town. I am sick and tired of German guys in leather shorts and French gals in tight blouses!" Greg and Bill were a little taken aback as Angelo was a rather gentle guy who did not normally blow off a head of steam like this.

Bill, a little bit saltier than the other two, responded by challenging Angelo in a fast clip typical of the way these good buddies talked to each other "Where the hell would you like to go, Angelo?"

Not skipping a beat, Angelo replied "Let's go to the place of our origins….the land of Byzantium…..Constantinople!" Especially important since all three of them were descendants of people from the Byzantine Empire which later became part of the Ottoman Empire.

And Greg added "Let's go first class on the Orient Express!" The very next day they left Athens for Thessaloniki where they boarded the fabled Orient Express as it arrived from Paris and headed on to the mysterious city of Istanbul which bridged that very narrow body of water between Europe and Asia.

They quickly found the "Oriental Compartment" that was to be their living and sleeping quarters for their overnight trip to the magic city of Istanbul.

As soon as they boarded the train, exuberantly appeared their "very special" Steward who was to take care of them for their journey. "My name is Bartok and I am here to serve you," he announced in clear but accented Greek words signifying that he was probably a Balkan but there was no way to determine exactly what

kind of a Balkan he was. Bartok searched through his repertoire of several other languages before establishing Greek as the language he would use to discuss matters with his guests.

His Greek was so natural that even Angelo, who was the best Greek speaker of the three, accepted him as being of Greek heritage somehow. Bill Crassas thought Bartok was a very charming guy whereas Angelo Kalaris viewed him with suspicion since he personified the "pouneros" (clever) manner of that part of world.

Greg Parkos was a little preoccupied with a young lady passenger in the next compartment, who paid him no attention at all but did seem interested in Bill. She was also on her way to Istanbul and their vision of an oriental tryst was quickly dispelled when she mentioned her Turkish lover was awaiting her at the Pera Palas.

171

Walking along the corridor to their compartment Bartok carried the bags and whispered to them that he would provide his new found friends with the benefits of his skill and knowledge especially about the Turks as he put it. This was a sleeper train and it was rather late in the evening so after depositing the three with their baggage in their compartment, Bartok disappeared and returned within minutes with a bottle of wine and some bedtime snacks for them. And then, glancing up and down the corridor, he whispered his secret, winking at Bill and holding Greg's arm, to suggest an alliance of friends. He aimed his pitch to Angelo who continued to look at him with a doubting eye.

He told them the Turks had an official exchange rate of only 1 Turkish Lira for each American dollar whereas he, as a good friend now, was able to give them 3 Turkish Liras for that same dollar. But, he said, he would have to do it before we reached the Turkish border so that he would not get into trouble with the law. Bill and Greg agreed to have him exchange $50 for each of them and they secreted the ill-gotten gains in their pockets smiling that they had such an advantage by having Bartok as their steward. Angelo did not trust Bartok so he did not participate. The next mid-day upon arriving in Istanbul, they tipped Bartok generously for being so good to them.

  Their first stop after leaving the train station was the Pera Palas, the hotel made famous because Agatha Christie wrote her book "Murder on the Orient Express" there. They had a glass of Raki in the Orient Express Bar and toasted their arrival in this city of enchantment, Constantinople.

Swiftly grabbing a taxi to their hotel, The Istanbul Hilton, the newest hotel in the city, they went directly to the rooms with the help of a young bell-man who was gregarious and extremely courteous. After he dropped off the bags and just before he left, he turned and said "The official Turkish exchange rate is not very realistic in the real world so if any of you wish to exchange your dollars for Turkish lira, I will give you 10 Liras for every American dollar." Bill Crassas and Greg Parkos turned and looked at Angelo Kalaris with an apologetic "You were right, Angelo, about Bartok." Just one more Balkan crook!

Ready to party, Bill booked a table for them at the hotel's fancy dining room where a Russian group was entertaining that evening and the billing suggested a lot of exotic dancing, singing and fun for all.

It was time to dress up in American summer class style and the party boys (at that time Greg's age was 25, Bill and Angelo were 27) posed at the Istanbul Hilton Hotel for their "Istanbul" photo:

Greg Parkos   Angelo Kalaris   Bill Crassas

As they entered the formal dining room, the maitre d' guided them to a table right near the stage area so they would have an unobstructed view of the show. As they were studying the menu and sipping on some Turkish Raki with a dash of water, the first act of the Russian show started right in front of their table....it was a line of about 6 Cossack dancers who were almost constantly squatting and kicking up their heels to the exhilarating sound of Russian Music.

Greg got so excited by the music and the dancing that he decided to order something from the menu that he did not know just because it sounded exciting and seemed to fit the mood of the performance....it was "Steak Tartare." He expected that it would probably be served with spurts of flames dancing all around the dish just based on his excitement from having watched the Cossacks dance and the very explosive name of the dish. Angelo and Bill ordered the traditional Turkish dish called Imam Baldi. When the waiter placed the platter in front of Greg his first observation was that something was missing.....on the plate was a mound of finely chopped raw beef and on the side were dishes of onions, capers, and other seasoning....but nothing was cooked.

Looking at the plate carefully, Greg patiently waited for someone to come cook the raw meat so that he could eat it....but no one came so he had to conclude he was supposed to eat it in the state it was delivered. Carefully, with an overwhelming dose of condiments, Greg started to eat the outside edges of this mound of raw meat. Oh well, he thought, perhaps the Turks are as barbarian as some have described them and he pledged to never again order anything that he did not know, which pledge he violated rather regularly and with abandon as soon as he survived the cannibalistic dining event this particular evening.

The next day they traveled in a small caique boat to the old part of the city, Sultanhamet, and immediately entered the famous Covered Bazaar (Kapelicasse) to visit the famous merchants and see what they were selling.

Angelo and Greg were taken with a half-lira sovereign gold coin commemorating Abdul Hamid, Sultan of the Ottomans, mounted on a simple gold ring.

After bargaining for a pair of these little finger rings from the

asking price of $250 dollars in a series of rigorous offers and counter-offers including the entire range of drama of the "Baksi Trading" phenomena of the Near East which included hand gestures and regular threats to break off discussions, they settled on a final cash price of $60 for each one.

They decided to walk back to the hotel and take in some of the seaside views of the city including the docks where their predecessors boarded the boats to seek their fortunes elsewhere that took them away from this native country.

The local scenes had not changed very much it was apparent.

And then they passed over a foot bridge to climb the hill joining lots of folks on their evening walk home.

They spent a restful night at the hotel in happy preparation for their early departure the next day.

They were eager to get back on the Orient Express and settle scores with Bartok, the Balkan crook, however when they approached their car, it was obvious the their new Steward was another guy, so their opportunity to get revenge was lost. The memories of a fantastic trip to Byzantium, though, would be with them forever.

"I was thinking.....Vignettes of a Life Well Spent"

ONE WITHOUT ICE

Maybe about fifty times or so
over the past four years a ritual has
been forged to end the evening with a
nightcap at the bar of the Hotel
Telegrafo whenever visiting the old
city of Havana in Cuba.
Sipping fine Rum is the best way to
recall the events of the day just ended
and begin the process of clearing the
mind for new history to begin tomorrow again.

This particular night was just a little bit unusual in that as the
circle of friends began to narrow as time went by, the bar staff started
taking up some of the patter of conversation that always accompanied
this ritual. Pedro was behind the bar preparing drinks, Ambrose was
the waiter, and Alexis was our guide and group raconteur.

The music ended, and still there were about a half dozen folks
sitting at a few scattered tables with the soft sound of laughter and
cheerfulness. My friend and I were at a small table near the end of
the bar so I strolled up to the edge of the bar where Pedro, Ambrose,
and Alexis were engaged in conversation to order a last drink.

To get their attention I spoke up "Ambrose, bring us two doubles
of the best Santiago aged rum and put ice in one of them, please."
Playing along with the happy spirit of our relationship, Ambrose
responded "which one of you wants the glass with the ice in it?"

"You figure it out, Ambrose, I never in my life have used a
condom" was my reply. After I returned to the table, Ambrose and
his buddies brought the drinks and placed the glass of Rum without
ice in front of me. I lifted the glass and drank it without hesitation
causing an eruption of laughter around the table except, of course, for
my tablemate who did not know what was happening.

"I was thinking.....Vignettes of a Life Well Spent"

PAPOU

From where I stood, he was a big man, almost gigantic and all-powerful. Later in life, I learned that he was ordinary in height maybe about 5 foot 8 inches tall and a bit on the stout side, say 225 lbs, but he was monumental to me, his first grandchild, and I knew he loved me.

He came to live with us in Newport about 1936 when I was six years old and we had just moved into the second floor tenement at 82 Thames with an attic upstairs that was made over into a bedroom for my maternal grandfather "papou"....an intimate Greek word meaning grandfather.

He was always special to me and I always called him by this intimate name that became so infectious in its sound that everyone in our home town who knew him and my relationship with him would call him "papou" or sometimes just plain "Pop" and I loved him as much as he loved me. We were close.

Papou was a gambler and he loved to play the "numbers" with the local bookies and cards at the Greek-American coffee shop upstairs over a store in a side street of Newport. The numbers are a very popular method of gambling for working people in poor neighborhoods...for example an individual would choose a series of 3 numbers such as 519 and then he would bet maybe 10 cents that the number would come out in that exact order and perhaps another 5 cents that it would be a combination of those numbers and the bookie would write your bet down on a pad as follows: 10-519-5.

If the number came in as 519 then the payoff of exact order bet would be 600 to 1 which meant $60 on the 10 cent bet....on the other bet referencing the combination then if , for example, the number was 195 then the payoff was something like 100 to 1 or 5$ on the 5 cent bet.

The number each night at 5 p.m. was selected in two ways…the last 3 digits of the U.S. Treasury balance which was published by the Government each day in the Boston newspaper, the Daily Record which arrived in town each day at about that time, the betting having been cut off several hours earlier, or by the throwing of a "die" at the local gambling backroom upstairs over the Narragansett Bar on Long Wharf.

My papou took me to see that event one day with the permission of the local gambling boss, John McCann, and it was marvelous. There was a pool table in the middle of the room that was nice and clean with a single 10 sided die (one of a pair of dice) placed at one edge.

At exactly 5 p.m. someone, on this night it was me who had the honors at the advanced age of 9 years old, would toss the die 3 times and that would establish the order and the numbers for that day. There were about two dozen men in attendance and that certainly insured honesty.

Papou made a fortune gambling and lost a fortune gambling.

I loved him so much and sometimes even now when I approach his final age, I can feel his arms around me and his scratchy one day old growth of beard as he kissed my right cheek vigorously….especially on those melancholy nights when I remember our kitchen table.

For me growing up, my mother's kitchen table was the center of the universe. When I next see her, I know she will invite me to sit down at the kitchen table while she hovers over me. And Dad will be demanding that she run and get me something to eat. Then, Papou will grab me and kiss me on my right cheek with that day old growth of beard.

I was loved!

PAPOU'S FAREWELL

One Sunday morning in December 1953, Teddy left home early to open the Supreme Lunch as he normally did on every morning of the year. On this particular day he was a little slower since he and Mary had spent the previous night at a Greek Church dance at Easton's Beach Pavilion. Mary was awake to see him off but all the kids were sleeping in that morning and not going to Church.

Bill Moss, the Cop on the beat, entered the restaurant at about midmorning and took Teddy aside for a short conversation, after which Teddy jumped into his car and headed out.

Mary was surprised and maybe even shocked to see Teddy returning home before noontime while she was in the living room folding laundry. He walked directly toward her, held out his arms and lifted her into an embrace while softly saying "Mary, I am sorry but Papou died this morning on the front steps of the Church."

Now that Mary's kids were all home for a short time at least, Papou had moved to his daughter Sophie's home and when he prepared to go to Church that Sunday no one was awake to drive him. Being of a dedicated nature and easily angered, Papou decided to walk to Church on his own. As he walked up the front steps of the Church his heart failed him and he collapsed expelling his last breath halfway up the staircase.

Mary's sadness was especially deep. She cared for her father since her Mother's death during the Black Plague of 1918. Feeling orphaned again for the second time and trembling, Mary collapsed.

Teddy placed her on the sofa where they sat in each other's arms and cried for they had lost the only parent they had known together and their children had lost their only Grandparent.

"I was thinking…..Vignettes of a Life Well Spent"

PAPOU'S SECRET

My grandfather was a fabulous guy. When he would laugh, his whole body would join in the excitement. Everyone called him Papou, which meant Grandfather in the Greek vernacular.

One of the most moral and ethical men I had ever known and he was held in the highest regard by all. As I knew him, he was a cook and had always lived with us….it was like having a second father in the house. His wife had died when he was just about 38 years of age and he never was with another woman throughout his whole life. She was the only woman he had known and he mourned her for more than 35 years until his death.

When he approached his seventies about 1950 he used to kid around with me that since I was his oldest grandson, he had a secret he needed to share with me before his death. It had to be revealed for his redemption, he said, and he seemed a little serious about it even if it was said in a jovial way.

I went off to University and served in the Army and later as I was awaiting an assignment abroad where I would serve for the next three years, I reminded my Papou of his wish and he shared the secret with me. Now, I record it for you and for all that follow.

Along about 1907, Stelios Diomandes was a 27 year old young man who had not really carved out a life role for himself in the village of Kerassia, Turkey. A good man, but without a serious purpose yet in life.

He adored a pretty young 18 year old girl of the village named Styliani and she seemed to respond to his glances and subtle overtures.

When he approached her family for permission to marry her, they refused because he did not have the means to take care of a family.

Despite this rejection, he continued to court the young lady in his own way with furtive looks and light banter. Her responses were positive so he dared to meet with her out of sight of the villagers in the fields of fruit that surrounded the small village. A series of these meeting ended in their agreement that they were in love with one another so he approached the family again and was, once again, refused not because of character but because he did not have means or a way to achieve things.

The lovers were despondent an therefore decided to take action into their own hands, so my Papou made love to this young maiden and impregnated her with the child that would become my mother. My mother was conceived out of wedlock.

Of course, this turn of events resulted in a very quick marriage in the village. As he told this story, I could see a glint of mischief in my grandfather's eyes as he laughed and giggled while reciting the tale. How wonderful this story was to my ears.

He had his way...he won his one true love in life...and they created my mother who made my life wonderful in her love.

Thank you, Papou.

"I was thinking…..Vignettes of a Life Well Spent"

PARIS IN THE WINTER SUN

It is the last days of February in 1999 and soon I will be finishing my 69th year since birth but what a glorious feeling I have today as I sit on the Eurostar train with a can of Budweiser in my hand and a mozzarella and tomato sandwich on the table as my mind drifts back to the last 24 hours with January in Paris…and even further to a Springtime some 46 years ago when I first visited the City of Lights on my way home.

I was 26 years old then and my January is now 21 years old and she has all the savvy and awareness that I had at the same time and even quite a bit more. Her life will be as much a progression from where I left off as mine was from my Father's ending.

Tragic that I will not see it progress just as my Father did not see what I did with his gift to me.

As we walked the boulevard on this Sunday approaching the Place de Bastille we encountered an open market day under the winter sun.

A few luscious black olives, a good sized piece of cheese, a crusty loaf of break and a bunch of bananas…it was as natural as breathing to shop for these few items for January to take to her apartment.

And then to sit on the square for a baguette and a glass of red wine while we watched Paris stroll by….a Father and his Daughter, with whom he was well pleased.

"I was thinking…..Vignettes of a Life Well Spent"

PASSING FANCY

Have you ever met a woman, not prettier than others, but with an essence that pulls you into her web of attraction? And yet, she cannot be yours! You know that up front and you believe and trust that is true no matter what! Sometimes it happens when you just glanced and her quiet face without emotion said "Hi, There."

A memory I treasure….so what! Nothing happened, not even a kiss or the touching of hands but a soft warm feeling whenever I glanced about and saw her face. And when she was not in view, the glow of anticipation shadowed the fear that she would not return.

There was no evidence that she even felt the same way but that did not matter because it was my personal emotion that I was dealing with. Laughter, chatter, glimpses, reaching out for a touch, a kiss on the hand blew into the air….but no true suggestion of a relationship. Was it real or was it the setting and my imagination?

And then it ended. It was over and yet it never even really began….a singular devotion to an idea and feeling that had no echo…and with a sigh I had to turn and walk away.

Alone in the stillness of solitude, I looked into the night sky from my perch and thought of her. Isn't that a pretty thought? Maybe for another lifetime, if there is such a thing.

It was not just her devotion to another , it was also my devotion to another. She had no name? She mattered not? Nor did I? It was over and yet it never started. Adios! Call me when you get to heaven. Maybe we can talk again…sweet thing.

I climbed the stairs, the dream was over and there were other matters to deal with as I prepared to fix that which was unbroken and take center stage for the rest of this play called "My Life."

PATIENCE AND HOPE

There was a young girl in my life many years ago, 40 or so years as a matter of fact, and I had kind of lost touch with her...but recently on the occasion of my 71st birthday she called to learn about me and it was good to hear from the past. She told me that she had recently quoted an old story of mine to make a point about being patient and hoping for a brighter future.

It took me a few minutes to remember such a story in my repertoire but it finally came to me....it was this story...which she asked me to repeat:

In a long ago Kingdom, there were two Gypsies who were found guilty of stealing and brought before the King for sentencing.

The first Gypsy was named Taraf and he pleaded for his life but the King refused clemency and ordered him to be put to death.

The second Gypsy, Sorba, spoke to the King before he could be sentenced.

Sorba said "Your Majesty, spare my life and within one year I will teach your horse to speak." The King was bemused and decided to accept this challenge but cautioned that if the horse did not speak in one year that Sorba would die.

When they were lead away, Taraf turned to Sorba and said "Are you crazy, there is no way you can teach that horse to speak" to which Sorba replied:

"In one year, the King could die...or...I could die...or...the horse could talk."

The teaching? Be hopeful, be optimistic, time is an important weapon in this battle called life. The Universe is unfolding as it should, but it does not hurt to skip a beat every once in a while to catch your breath.

"I was thinking.....Vignettes of a Life Well Spent"

PLACE OF BIRTH

Between the Bosporus and the Dardanelles on the North bank of the Sea of Marmara, my parents were born in the little village of Kerassia in the Ottoman Empire. A pretty place but hopelessly poor where one made his living from the soil growing fruit...except for the brickyard.

The brickyard was right on the shore of the Sea and the village was about 1 kilometer from it at a relatively sharp incline upward. The morning walk to work was cheerful and good-natured as the men walked downhill but the afternoon walk home after 10 hours of work was labored and difficult.

It was easier to work in the fields and that is what most of the residents did and especially since their women and children could work alongside them. This improved productivity provided a means for the menfolk to be able to avoid work whenever they felt like visiting the village center, which they did often, to just sit and talk with the other men in the coffee shops.

My paternal Grandfather Kyriakos chose the brickyard, as had his father before him. Kyriakos and his father worked in the area where the bricks were fired and as a consequence called "the brick baker" by the villagers.

The individual brick was a work of art itself as each one had molded on the face a picture of a 3 masted schooner which I must presume was meant to reference the fact that the bricks were made on the edge of the sea. The backside of the brick displayed the name of the yard and the name of nearest town, Myriofiton, in Greek letters. The lettering on the brick was  in the Greek language despite being made in a Turkish factory and must, I presume, have been necessary to allow it to be marketable beyond the local limits into further reaches of the Mediterranean.

Between the Bosporus and the Dardanelles, my soul was born and I am a child of that region almost as surely as if I were born there.

QUEEN OF CALCUTTA

Under cover of darkness, they slipped out of Perth on the West Coast of Australia and headed through the Indian Ocean on a zig-zag path for the Bay of Bengal and Calcutta, their target destination.

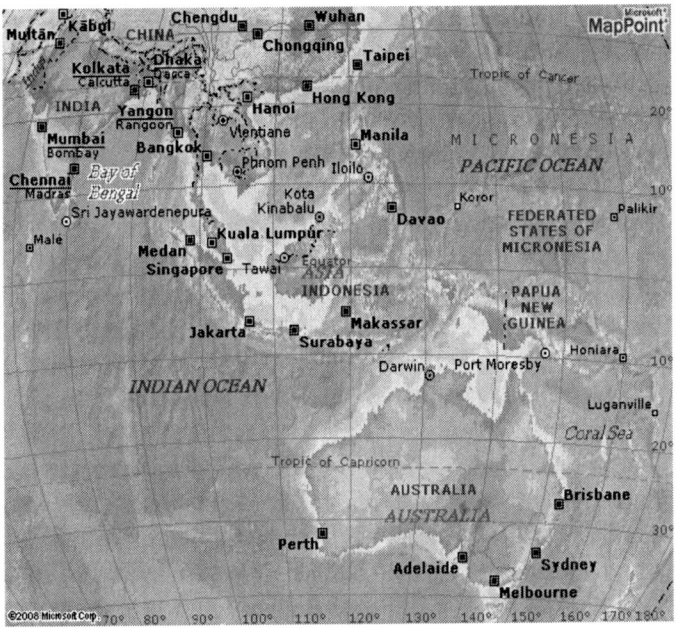

The voyage would take almost a week and this was after the band of fifteen American O.S.S. agents had spent more than ten days crossing the Pacific. These highly trained guerilla leaders, who were to eventually lead Kachin tribesmen behind the Japanese lines in Burma, were all Greek-Americans being assigned to the 101st O.S.S. Detachment in the China-Burma-India Theatre of Operations in World War II.

But this is not a war story. Heroic men never tell war stories; they only recite the follies of their ordinary human ways in strange times and places. That is what makes them such extraordinary people.

The Bay of Bengal was a shooting gallery for the Japanese who controlled the entire East coast of that waterway and the probability of their making it all the way to Calcutta was not very high.

But, they did make it. Exhausted and feeling caged in like animals on that small boat, they jumped onto the dock in Calcutta. Within a matter of just a few hours they were cleaned up and dressed in clean uniforms on their way into the city of Calcutta where they split up to find various forms of entertainment.

One gang of four included Dan Diomandes, who was the oldest of the group at 29 and the only one married, as well as an old family friend of his, Ralph Stratis. Dean Brelis, a Harvard educated Officer, and Ernie Tsikerdanos, rounded out the group. A British colleague suggested that they visit the "Sonagachi" district just north of the Marble Palace, where he recommended a place named "Golden Tree."

The area had been used by the Bengali Babus for maintaining concubines and mistresses in the 1800s. Remnants of that atmosphere still existed in the neighborhood. The guys entered this majestic looking Victorian house which had an elaborate parlor just inside the front door vestibule. The furniture in the room was predominantly red velvet upholstered with lots of elaborate mirrors on the wall.

The hostess, named Mary, spoke first to Dean Brelis since she recognized that he was the highest ranking one and invited him and his colleagues to sit by the fireplace on a pair of love seats which faced each other. Playing a piano in the corner was an older gentleman wearing an elaborate Indian outfit. Mary served them their famous house specialty, Gin and Tonic. And, a young girl dressed in a Sari served them small dishes of food treats.

Something was a little different in the room to these guys as they perused that there was an unusual number of separate ladies sitting alone at different locations throughout the rather large room. Dean Brelis turned toward Dan Diomandes and said "God damn it, Danny, I think we are in a fancy Bordello whore house!" Dan responded that he would be happy to just sit there, eat, drink and enjoy the music since he was married and who would not cheat on his wife.

Dan was kind of having fun at this point and pointed to a large painting over the mantle of the fireplace which displayed the Acropolis of Athens on top of the Parthenon. "Hey, Mary, why that scene rather than the Taj Mahal?" he asked. "Because I am a Greek" said Mary.

The rest of the evening was spent in Greek banter, food, and drink between these four buddies and their hostess but to the best of our historic records no other business was conducted that night.

They left at midnight and Mary refused to let them pay anything for their libations. Her only request was that each one of them please remember her when they saw the enemy in their gunsight and say "This one is for Mary, the Greek Madame of "Sonagachi."

These guys did not forget their promise to the lady they called the "Queen of Calcutta." Unfortunately, Ralph was a casualty of war even before their mission in a tragic accident while training. Dean, Dan and

Ernie, however, went on to honor her request within a very short time after they parachuted into Burma behind the Japanese lines to lead Kachin tribesmen. Each one of them paid their agreed-to tab for that night in Calcutta.

189

"I was thinking.....Vignettes of a Life Well Spent"

RAINBOW SIGN

"And God gave Noah the Rainbow Sign,
No More Water,
The Fire Next Time"

That line from an old Negro spiritual comes to mind when I remember flying into Pamplona to run with the bulls for the feast of St Fermin. Just as the small plane from Madrid was banking to land at the little airfield, off to the right I saw that rainbow sign. It is funny about rainbows, you kind of have to look at a particular angle to pick up the colors.... but it happened that day. July 5th. My mother's birthday.

It wasn't the first time that I had experienced a new adventure on the anniversary of her birth, remembering that I visited the village of her birth for the first time on that special day also. My Mom visits with me a lot especially in the last 23 years since she died.

The excitement of having achieved a life long dream to be in Pamplona for this Fiesta just took over my entire being starting on that day. Quickly, I slipped into my white linen pants and shirt as soon as I was at the hotel and dashed down the stairs and right into the old city to purchase my red sash and neckerchief to complete the outfit. I had arrived! Nadine thought I was insane but when she sensed the joy in my heart, she humored my eccentricity.

On the eve of this 8 day fiesta, we ventured just outside the hotel in the old city to feel the excitement. In my heart I was young again and happy and adventurous and filled with visions of delight. The bands of young people dressed exactly as I was dressed walked along these narrow old streets singing their songs with joy and drinking their Rioja with gusto.... it was fun.

Then, very suddenly, they caught sight of me. Dressed in white linens with flowing scarlet red adornments and my white beard I became the target of their attention.

They were about a dozen and all of a sudden they started toward me with their fingers pointing and they began to chant "Hem...ing...way" "Hem...ing...way" "Hem...ing...way" ; over and over again. They were saluting my appearance as kind of a reincarnation of the hero of the Running of the Bulls, Ernesto. They embraced us with wine and song and the Fiesta began that moment and lasted continuously for 8 straight days.

On the first morning after our arrival, we went down to the corrals to see if I could run with the bulls that morning. The crowds were so thick around the course that I could not get into the corrals to run, so we went down to the bullring where that day's bulls came into the arena after the running. It was exciting...there were a dozen bulls from which the 6 to be fought that night were chosen. This ritual was repeated every day of the fiesta. The rest of the day was spent with crowds of people everywhere we went just singing, laughing and enjoying the festivities. There were young people, old folks, entire families...everyone in white and red looked fantastic.

After the traditional late afternoon siesta to sleep off some of the champagne and weariness, we strolled along the old streets again toward the arena listening to the continuing chant of "Hem...ing...way" wherever I went and there were bands and marching groups everywhere. We reached the arena and found our seats which were well placed in a group of older local folks who seemed to know each other and were exuberant when greeting each other.  It was very comfortable to be in their midst. Across the arena on the other side mostly was occupied by young people with colorful jackets representing their various clubs.

Their excitement added a lot to the festival.

Then came the fights. Handsomely groomed bullfighters and ferocious looking bulls faced off against each other. Let the games begin! I had seen many bullfights in the past so I knew the rituals well but for Nadine it was a new experience with ups and downs and everything in between. There are 6 bulls and 3 matadors who perform each evening. After the 3rd matador had fought his first bull, something happened at Pamplona that I had never experienced before. It was like a 7th inning stretch in American baseball.

All these elegantly dressed and joyful older folks, with whom we were sitting, started opening their handbags and brought forth a cornucopia of plenty. Meats, cheeses, sandwiches and loads of wine in leather containers. These absolute strangers started pushing their offerings into our hands and insisted that we share everything despite our hesitations. Their laughter and embraces were contagious and before we knew it, we were drinking and eating as if we were lifelong friends with these folks.

A lesson well learned. The next night and every night after that we would go shopping before going to the arena so that we also had offerings to share with them.

What a happy time we had with our new friends….the gentle people of Pamplona. And after the fights, off to a restaurant for a stew made from the tail of the bull and paella and always lots of Rioja to drink.

The most fantastic 8 days I could have imagined.

Mi Llama "Hem…Ing…Way". Muchas Gracias!

"I was thinking…..Vignettes of a Life Well Spent"

SASSY AND ME

Never did like my birthdays…too self conscious for the attention required of others to make a fuss about me and this year was certainly not any different. It was 1950 and it was March 11 and it was a Saturday night with nothing to do but study for the Monday exams in my $5 a week room on Williams Street, Providence. And, not enough dough in my pocket to choose many alternatives to my state of being so I went out to eat at one of the cheapest places I knew nearby.

The local "greasy-spoon" Louis Restaurant was a favorite for me in those days and I was able to feast on a large platter of spaghetti and meatballs for just a half-buck. Louis, the owner, who had just migrated to America from Italy was, as always, very animated and waxing excitedly about the vocal style of a gal singer's new song on his juke box called "The Nearness of You." As she softly filled the restaurant with those beautiful lyrics and the sweetest vocal sound I had ever heard, I dwelled on the words:

Its not the pale moon that excites me
That thrills and delights me, oh no
Its just the nearness of you
It isn't your sweet conversation
That brings this sensation, oh no
Its just the nearness of you
When you're in my arms
and I feel you so close to me
All my wildest dreams come true
I need no soft lights to enchant me
If you'll only grant me the right
To hold you ever so tight
And to feel in the night the nearness of you

Just then, the guy sitting next to me at the counter turned and told Louis that the singer was performing that night at a new Jazz nightclub downtown called the Celebrity Club in Randall Square.

193

I jumped off the stool, paid my bill and started walking down College Hill and within about twenty minutes I was standing in front of The Celebrity Club, a brightly lit place in the middle of a black neighborhood. It was a small supper club that had fifteen tables in the main dining area and a small bar off to the left with about a dozen stools running from the front of the place right up to within a few feet of the stage. The big guy at the door introduced himself to me as Paul Fillipi, the owner. When I asked Paul if I could sit at the bar for a drink to watch the show, he pointed to the end of the bar that was closest to the stage and said "Go ahead, kid, sit right there."

The bartender took my order for a bottle of Narragansett Beer which I figured had to be the cheapest drink in the joint and cheerfully with a warm tone took my dollar bill and returned three quarters next to my glass. Obviously pleased that I had chosen such a cheap drink, I swung around on my stool so I could face the stage. Sucking on that single beer for what seemed to be an endless period of time, I sensed a special quiet amongst the roomful of people in the audience….and the spot lights came on.

Then Paul Fillipi walked to the microphone and announced "Ladies and Gentlemen, I present to you tonight the most wonderful and incomparable young jazz lady, the Sassy one… Sarah Vaughan. She started singing "It's Magic" and I feel in love with this lady who was later to be titled "The Divine One" by a then Chicago disk jockey named Dave Garroway.

After the show, the bartender, with whom I had become friendly, signaled Sassy to come to the bar and he introduced me saying: "This college boy is in love with you." She put her hand on my cheek then walked away saying

"Thanks, Lover Boy, you be good."

"I was thinking.....Vignettes of a Life Well Spent"

SATURDAY NIGHT GIRLS

It started in the fall of 1942 and they were always in groups of two or three or four, but never a single one alone, arriving by six in the early evening on Saturday nights. They were all working girls from towns neighboring the city of Newport, like Fall River and Providence. Newport was where the boys were as it was a training center for thousands of young sailors. Back in the home towns of these girls, the "boys next door" had all gone off to war themselves and were stationed at distant locations around the World.

A caravan of Shortline Bus Company vehicles would drop them off in Washington Square right in front of the Army-Navy YMCA just in time for the weekly dance in the large open recreation hall on the main floor. Some tall, some short, some wide, some thin...but somehow they all looked alike in some funny kind of way. ...lots of makeup and plenty of costume jewelry adorning tight fitting tops and wearing wide smiles on their beaming faces. All the Saturday Night Girls were in their late teens or early twenties and eager to have fun.

The boys at the Army-Navy YMCA were young sailors. The old sailors did not visit there as it was not on the route they took to get to the bars where more seasoned ladies of the evening awaited them.

The dancing started early and after a few hours some groups of Saturday Night Girls accompanied by Sailor Boys would peel off to go visit the Supreme Lunch up the street on Broadway for hamburgers, French fries and soda pop. Then back for another hour of dancing before catching the midnight shuttle bus back to their home towns. Often, they returned to meet with the same boys or meet new sailors since their former had gone off to war.

A few of the daring Saturday Night Girls headed to the Blue Moon Café or the Bohemian Garden to spend late hours watching strippers while drinking with older sailors and arranging to spend the night in Newport with "Friends."

195

"I was thinking…..Vignettes of a Life Well Spent"

SIX IN THIRTY SIX

"It was the best of times….." and how I relished 1936 as my sixth year of life with so many wonderful things happening to my family.

First, my father got a regular job. After a year of working on fishing boats for a share of the catch and a year of public works projects with the W.P.A. (that super concept of government during the depression which put able persons to work doing public works for modest pay and food supplements but left their dignity intact…but more on that in another essay), my Dad got a job with the City of Newport as the night watchman in the city yard, where the gravel and sand were stored at the end of Long Wharf in the heart of the city. His pay was $ 36 per week…interesting number!

Second, we moved from 13 Poplar Street where we lived in a poorly maintained, run down second floor tenement in the poor folks area of "the Point" to a larger and more openly lighted second floor tenement at 82 Thames Street nearer to Washington Square which was the center of town. The difference was remarkable. We had an upstairs attic to explore our fantasies and to play for hours on end in comforting privacy. The rent was $36 per month…that same number!

Third, my brother and I were joined by a baby sister, Estelle, that seemed to make our family more complete in my mind and I was thrilled with the added love that this addition caused amongst all of us as this tiny baby took shape and form over the holidays.

Fourth, I had finished my first year of school at Calendar School where the kindergarten teacher, Miss. Gleason, took a Greek speaking frightened little boy and turned him into an American youngster.

My relationship with Miss. Gleason lasted for the rest of her long life and I idolized the kindness and gentleness of this lovely woman. My next school was Potter Street school and that was just fine to start anew with a new personality at a new school and my brother, John, took my place with Miss. Gleason.

Fifth, my Grandfather "papou" (my mother's father) came to live with us together with his daughter, my Aunt Sophie, from the Boston area and our family exploded almost overnight from four to five and then to seven….it was wonderful! Aunt Sophie helped with the new baby and the other household chores while working and bringing her salary into the household as was my dear Papou. The house we lived in became a home for three generations of family.

Sixth, I learned about the gift of love that year because at Thanksgiving time we found a gift on the hall landing outside the door to our tenement…a large basket of food for our family from the local chapter of the Knights of Columbus. Heading the team of men was a man I knew as Eli Lahoud and I was taken (and still am) with the fact that a Roman Catholic Church organization was that kind to a family that subscribed to another religion…for we were Greek Orthodox. About ten years later I saw this same man, Eli Lahoud, perform a great act of courage by himself but that is another story and I won't forget to tell it.

The depression had been hard and we were finally seeing a little light at the end of the tunnel and the year of 1936 ended gloriously when John and I were invited to a Christmas party at the Salvation Army hall which they sponsored for poor and disadvantaged children…lots of fun, some good things to eat, songs to sing, and most important of all…lots of love to share.

God bless you all. I remember your kindness all the days of my life and in keeping with your magnificent obsession; I try to do the same to others.

"I was thinking…..Vignettes of a Life Well Spent"

SLEEPING WITH ODYSSEUS' WIFE

I had just turned 24 years old and was newly arrived in Athens. Before undertaking my duties in the American Mission to the Balkans my country chief sent me to Cephalonia to help with relief efforts.

A series of four earthquakes had hit the island and caused major destruction with virtually every house on the island destroyed. My role was to assist the thousands of people who were seeking a new life elsewhere. The USA considered them to be eligible to immigration to America under the Refugee Relief Act even though the primary goal of that legislation was to help the victims of the Communist insurrection which lead to a five year civil war in Greece.

From Patras I took a small boat and landed on the island to find that there was no place to house me since every building was destroyed and the people were living in makeshift shelters and tents.

The Chief of Police on the island was so happy to see me that he quickly arranged temporary housing for me in a tent occupied by Odysseus Papadakos and his wife. But there were only two cots in the tent. They insisted that I use one of the cots during the night hours and Odysseus would use it to sleep during the daytime. His wife, of course, they explained, would sleep in the other cot during the nighttime. I followed the wife up the pathway that had been cut alongside the rubble to the place where the tent had been recently pitched. She was a typical woman of that region, dressed in black, with a scarf over her head and the aroma of garlic and body odors encircling her.

198

After a few hours of work with the Police near the harbor, I returned to the tent so I could get some sleep in preparation for the next day's rather full schedule of work. Odysseus was waiting for me outside the tent where he had set up a place for himself to sit out the nighttime hours. He insisted once again that I sleep on the cot in the next and said that his wife had already retired and was sound asleep. The time was about ten in the evening and it was quite dark except for a couple of kerosene lamps inside and outside the tent.

Every thirty minutes from the time I went to bed until sunrise, when I arose, Odysseus marched quietly through the tent in the space separating the two cots, which was only about four feet wide, up and back and then exit the tent. When I left them the next morning and thanked them for their hospitality, I asked Odysseus "By what name is your wife called?" and he answered "Penelope."

I suddenly realized that I was in the place that Homer had described as the homeland of the Greek hero "Odysseus" who returned from ten years of journey after the Trojans had been vanquished to confront and expel the suitors who had wooed his wife "Penelope."

Walking away from the tent, my mind went back to the ritual of the evening and somehow felt that perhaps I had become a player in the times of Greek mythology.

The journey to Cephalonia ended with great success and I returned to Athens to continue my original assignment but the memory of that night in Cephalonia still remains with me and I remember Odysseus and his Penelope.

"I was thinking…..Vignettes of a Life Well Spent"

SOPHIE'S BET ON 11225

Aunt Sophie often bet the numbers inspired by her dreams and sometimes she won but never understood why or even cared very much for the money. It was the thrill of winning that she desired.

Gambling in Newport was pretty common with plenty of bookies and if you did not know one, any cop would happily show you where the betting parlor was located upstairs over Chris Thompson's Newport Tavern on Long Wharf. A large center room with a table in the middle upon which a large ten sided numbered die was rolled every night at 5:00 P.M. first 3 times, then 4 times, and then again 5 times. If you had bet on 5 numbers and you got it right, the payoff was 600 to 1. For each dollar bet, you got $600 – a veritable fortune in those days.

Sunday, January 1, 1978 was an exhausting and exciting day in Aunt Sophie's life as she sat with her terminally ill sister Mary, my mother. They awaited news of the delivery of my first born child. It was as if they were enduring the labor cycle themselves because Mom just knew she would soon be leaving and that this new baby would be taking her place in my arms. Finally, I called with the news that the baby had arrived and we would be baptizing our baby with Mom's name in her honor. Aunt Sophie and Mom held each other and cried with joy, comparable to some 48 years earlier when they embraced each other that night that I was born at home on Princeton Street in Somerville. The next day, Aunt Sophie found her bookie and bet a buck on the number 11225 – because she had just dreamed it. She won $600 that night but had no explanation for why she played that number. Aunt Sophie gifted the baby her winnings explaining that she did not understand the number but that it meant something special about the baby. I then deciphered the number:

Mom's newest grandchild was born January 1 at 10:05 P.M.
First month, first day, twenty-second hour, fifth minute of the year.
Numerically stated: "11225"

AND NOW! (As Paul Harvey would say)
FOR THE REST OF THE STORY:

Mom's primary caretaker for her final years as she weakened and was wracked by cancer into a frail body was my sister Elaine, who had a truly unique insight into the events reported above.

It seems that some three or so months before the birth of the child an event occurred that Elaine recalls in her own words:

"Mumma awoke one morning and told me she had dreamed of the number 11225 and I should call Aunt Sophie to tell her to bet the number as she knew the procedure. I vividly remember calling Estelle and telling her about the number and speaking to her of the possibility that the number referred to Mumma's death. Would it be November 22? January 12????"

Did our mother forecast the exact time of her next grandchild's birth? And why this time rather than the many that preceded?

A simple story…Mom had five children and each one of them had given her grandchildren honoring her except, at this point in time, her first born…who was about to have his first child.

Not important enough for such a unique gift one might say, but let me add to that the fact that Mom knew that soon she would be leaving her family on this earth and was granted this last divine gift of insight to assure her of the passing from the last generation to the next.

It is written in Ecclesiastes:

"A generation goes, and a generation comes, but the earth remains forever."
"The sun rises and the sun goes down and hurries to the place where it rises."

201

SOPHIE'S CURE

Putrid was the English word but it w.... used in this household at 50 Tyler Street in Bosto... they only spoke Greek. The smell of Octagon soa... permeated the interior in an attempt to block out t... surrounding ugly smells. Family after family pac... into these tenements in the squalor of the inner cit... where the immigrants first went upon their arrival... America.

That was the world of the Diomandes family in February 1916 as they struggled to make their way in the New World. The tenement in which they lived near the top of the building housed a family of nine, who had departed from the village of Kerrasia, Turkey four years earlier.

There was the Grandmother, Smaragda, with her three single sons; Ioakim, Kyriakos, and Iosef; as well as her married son, Stergios, and his wife Styliani and their three children; Panagiota, Sophia, and Diomandes, the baby who had just celebrated his first birthday and had been named after his Grandfather from whom the family had taken their surname of Diomandes.

It was the custom of these Byzantine Greeks to live together as a family until marriage so the single brothers joined their married brother in working to support the family.

Their quarters were cramped so there was a lot of sharing. One bedroom housed Stergios and Styliani with their baby Diomandes, the second bedroom was for the Grandmother Smaragda, Panagiota and Sophia, and the three single brothers slept in the third bedroom. The beds they used were in the Ottoman style laid out on the floor with no legs so they could fit everyone in their 3 separate bedrooms. A kitchen and a living room completed their tenement.

It was cold and dark in the tenement on this particular night so Sophia, who was 3 years old, and her older sister Panagiota, who was almost 8 years old, went to bed early while their Grandmother stayed in the living room with her sons. Panagiota laid down on the inside against the wall while Sophia took the outside position closer to the door.

A loud shriek from the girls' bedroom brought the whole family into that room to respond. Sophia was screaming and crying and jumping up and down holding her right hand with her left. She was hysterical and Panagiota was frightened for she did not know what had happened to her sister who had been sleeping beside her.

A rat had bitten her hand while she slept.

The family gathered to review their collective wisdom on what treatment would be appropriate to cure this disaster and, of course, Smaragda, being the elder, lead the discussion. The resolution was an old world cure that Smaragda remembered which was effective in somewhat similar situations so they agreed to take that course of action.

Sophia was to drink a small amount of her baby brother's urine and that would cure her injury.

She did and she was!

"I was thinking…..Vignettes of a Life Well Spent"

SOPHIE'S PICK

My guess is that it was about 1937, when I was 7 years old and she was 24, that our special love affair began and it was to last for another 55 years on this earth and will continue in my mind until I also close my eyes. She was my Aunt Sophie.

Although she had been at my birth and lived around the corner for the first 3 years of my life, I did not really know her until she came to Newport in the Fall of 1936 to live with us and to help my mother with the arrival of her third child, our sister Estelle.

It seems to me that Sophie was attractive in shape and form but I was not really aware of such things at that age. What I felt was a certain warmth and happiness when she would talk and tease with me. Sophie was a charmer. I was fascinated by the way she lived her life and her manner….so different than her sister, my mother.

During the winter following her arrival in Newport, Sophie started to participate in the social whirl of the small Greek Church in our home town. No debutante balls mind you, just the typical Greek socials at Christmas for dancing and laughing.

There were 3 young ladies in the social circuit that winter and they were all in their early twenties…the marrying age…and they were all in search of the young men of the town who were in their thirties.

The ladies were Mabel Fotelis and her sister, Effie, as well as my Aunt Sophie. The eligible men of the Greek community were Mike Papademetriou, George Sarellis, and George Alexander.

It seemed to me that Mabel had targeted George Alexander, her sister was chasing George Sarellis and Aunt Sophie was after Mike Papademetriou.

But, they were not exclusively committed to the individual and the chase was on between the ladies to get one of the three to ask for their hand in marriage…and it didn't matter which one. The Fotelis girls had a big advantage in that their father, Angelo Fotelis, owned a couple of restaurants and represented future security for the lucky man who won their hand. Aunt Sophie had her work cut out for her.

As I remember it George Sarellis was from the island of Lesbos, George Alexander was from the Greek mainland, and Mike Papademetriou was from the Island of Spetsis. The Fotelis family was also from Lesbos and Aunt Sophie's family was from Turkey (Eastern Thrace). The Greek instinct always is to marry your own kind therefore George Sarellis got his pick of the Fotelis girls and a lifetime job in their daddy's restaurant…he choose Effie.

The mating dance was a wonder to behold. I remember the funny stories. The 3 men because they were single lived in boarding houses and Mike had a room on Spring Street with a window on the sidewalk.
One day when he was calling on Aunt Sophie he mentioned that he awakened that morning to find a baked apple on his window sill. A gift from one of the Fotelis girls….Aunt Sophie blew her top and pouted about their using unfair tactics in the competition because they had money and that they were brazen to do such a thing. Really, she was just angry that she had not thought of it first.

It was not a serious problem to overcome for Aunt Sophie. She just tightened the belt a little more that day on her dress to emphasize the natural curve lines of her bodice…and Mike was almost panting. The ritual was so amazing for me to watch and so natural. She was the best teacher of "flirting" that any young boy could have wished.

But this was serious business and the whole family spent long hours talking about getting Aunt Sophie married. I think she preferred George Sarellis but he had already staked out the money in the Fotelis girl and shortly after that George Alexander made his move for the other Fotelis girl and the "job for life" in the restaurant.

205

That left Mike for Aunt Sophie. Her father, my Papou, was eager for Aunt Sophie to settle down; my mother wanted to see her happy; my father wanted her to leave; Mike wanted someone to take care of him; and Sophie wanted another kind of life.

Mike was a good looking young man with a wonderful figure. He was just above 6 feet tall with broad shoulders and a Tarzan like figure when he swam in the ocean, which he did every day that the weather permitted. His ritual was well known to me as my mother would make it a point to pack up my brother John and me and our baby Estelle along with Aunt Sophie to visit a little park named Battery Park on the waterfront where Mike performed his daily routine of a swim deep into the bay and then he would stretch out on an inclined rock that jutted out from the water about 50 feet from shore and sun bathe for a couple of hours or so. It was always the same. He would finish his sunning at about 4 in the afternoon and then head for work. He and his brother operated a restaurant together called the Apollo Lunch on lower Thames Street…where his brother worked days and Mike worked the night shift starting at 5 p.m. Mike was not devoted to work and not ambitious therefore it was always difficult for him every day when he had to leave his rock in the sun.

Mom's game was easy to understand and all the players knew it well. She brought some food for Mike and her sister, Sophie, to bring him some light humor. In some ways Mike preferred the food and graciousness of my mother to the light and happy ways of Sophie. So Sophie chooses Mike or maybe Mike choose Sophie, or more likely my father sat with Mike and arranged the whole thing since they were hunting buddies. It was "the right thing to do". But in the eyes of this little 7 year old, it was "the wrong thing to do".

Sophie's pick became part of our family. They got married and went off to the 1939 New York World's Fair for their honeymoon which was cut short so that Mike could get back to go hunting with Dad. The souvenir replica of the World Fair symbolic buildings was in Aunt Sophie's home for 50 years and it always bothered me.

"I was thinking.....Vignettes of a Life Well Spent"

STOMPING AT THE SAVOY

Late July is pretty busy in London. The tourists are everywhere and the sidewalk sounds like the Tower of Babel with the multitude of tongues being spoken. But I had a pretty easy time this visit nonetheless. Came in on Sunday (July 25, 1999) to be here for several days of meetings for Cookson but tonight was my own night and I contemplated the results as I sat at the Upstairs Bar eating my after Theatre dinner all alone.

The view from the bar where my particular preferred table is placed takes in the front door and even the Savoy Theatre, which is next door to the hotel. It is fun to watch them coming and going and to mentally envision who they are...Arab Princes, German Businessmen, American Movie Stars, British Peers...and then there is me.

Dad would not believe it. His first born son hanging out with all "The Swells" just "Stomping at the Savoy". And I feel like hell, just missing him. There is no question in my mind that my father thought I would do all right, but oh how I would have loved bringing him to London to hear the Doorman call out my name when I arrive with a car and driver..."Welcome back, again, Mr. Parkos". And then the same greeting from the bellman, and the receptionist and a personal greeting from the Manager in the Lobby..."It is nice to have you with us, Mr. Parkos?" Dad made up that name...I wish he could hear it called out with respect by that whole cadre at the Savoy.

What a miracle America is. In two generations from an oven tender in a brick factory on the shore of the Sea of Marmara to an independent Businessman in a small American City to what my Dad would have called a "big shot" pretending to be appropriately situated with the high and mighty at the Savoy. Actually, my Dad would have admonished me to humble myself and "stop posing for animal crackers".

The Theatre was wonderful (Hay Fever by Noel Coward), dinner was great, and the memory of sitting there with my Dad was divine. I lifted a glass of Champagne, French of course, and spoke a toast to the empty chair across from me..."Here's to you Teddy Parkos...and Thanks".

207

"I was thinking.....Vignettes of a Life Well Spent"

SUMMER ENTREPRENEUR

It was the summer of 1951 and as a newly minted MBA from Boston University; I knew that very soon I would be drafted into the Army to serve my country during the Korean War. It was expected that I, like my father before me, would serve my country and I was happy to do it. Despite this sense of duty, I still felt that I should wait to be called rather than volunteer. That is why I was waiting that summer with no idea of when I would be called but I knew it would not be more than a few months.

How to spend the summer? Why not do something useful like help a friend start a business? And that is how it started.

Ernie Bosas was an eager young Greek American from New Bedford who wanted to get into the restaurant business. He was a funny sort of chap, short and stocky but with a forward momentum to his body whenever he would walk…his short legs made it look more like he was dashing from place to place…and his jabber was continuous. At the end of every sentence almost without exception, his punctuation mark was the words "my friend" and you knew that it was such a meaningless expression from Ernie that it just about amounted to saying "you are not particularly of any interest to me".

Ernie had no money and no ideas so I decided to do my good deed for that year by arranging for him to become my partner in Teddy's Lunch on Thames Street. It had cost me $300 to buy the restaurant from Teddy and that was another story which is separately told.

Ernie and I decided that we would have to fix up the restaurant and rename it in order to make it look like a new business since the old Teddy's Lunch had become quite tired looking and dark on the inside. We took down the window curtains, cleaned the big storefront windows facing the Blue Moon Gardens across the street.

The Blue Moon was the only strip-tease joint in town and every night it was jammed full with sailors celebrating their liberty.

We outfitted the store with newly refurbished fixtures and furniture and put glaring neon signs in the two windows flashing brilliantly to the whole world that we were there. All of this from $1500.00 of credit from the restaurant fixture distributor in Fall River.

And then a new neon sign to hang over the front door announcing the "G & E Diner"....not imaginative but certainly ego-satisfying.

It was my philosophy that the diner should cater to the Navy crowd rather than the local citizens since they would more readily accept a new restaurant. The locals already had their favorite restaurants but the sailors were new in town and unattached.

We opened each day at 4:00 p.m. in the afternoon and closed at 4:00 a.m. in the morning...we were there for the sailors before and after their night of drinking and carousing at the Blue Moon Garden. The two young 17 to 18 year old girls that waited on the customers were certainly a positive influence on our business. Their personal inclinations to be camp followers did not hurt our business except that from time to time it became necessary to go by their apartments and get them out of bed in the afternoon to come in to work. Business was good all night long but after the strip-tease joint closed at 1:00 a.m., it just boomed almost every night. The drunken sailors with the few dollars they had falling out of their blouse pockets were certainly welcome at the G & E Diner.

The menu was simple. Our customers could choose from Chili or Hamburger Steak...maybe a few other items but nothing worth mentioning. The Juke box blared all night long and every nickel that went into it was ours to keep under a deal we made with the machine operator who also had placed a slot machine in our back hallway which was somewhat illegal, very lucrative, and shared between us on a 50/50 basis

At the end of our first week in August, we counted up the results of the restaurant business and the juke box and the slot machine and Ernie and I had $800.00 in cash to share. It was 1951 and that amount of money in cash was phenomenal.

Business kept up at that pace for the next few weeks and by mid September we had paid off all our debts when Ernie began to grumble. He started by complaining that he did the grill work and cooking while I spent my time serving the counter customers and talking to people. The diner had 4 booths and a counter with 8 stools so the serving staff of two waitresses and me was plentiful but you must remember that the two young lasses in the tight dresses were part of the entertainment for our customers.

As the griping got louder I suggested to Ernie that it was foolish for us to argue since I would be leaving for the service soon, it would be good for Ernie to buy me out now and let's separate as friends. He asked for my price and I suggested $1,500.00 which is about what my share had made in 4 weeks….he became angry and thought I was gouging him and suggested he would like to get $1,500.00 for his share and I accepted his challenge.

Now I owned 100% of the business and I had the sign immediately taken down and changed to "Greg's Town Diner" but nothing else changed, the menu stayed the same and the girls continued to shake their fannies and within a few weeks I had earned enough to pay off Ernie. As life unfolded Ernie continued to work in restaurants over the next 30 years before he died and he never again every earned as much per week as he had earned for those 8 weeks that he was my partner at the G & E. As a wise man told me later in life, no-one can ever do the damage to you that you can do to yourself. Ernie gave up a magnificent opportunity in life because he was petty…enough said.

By the middle of October I had $3,000.00 in my pocket in cash and no way to spend it. Each noontime when I would wake up I would go to the barber shop and get a shave and a face message and did other extravagant things when I could with the few hours I had free.

Working from 4:00 p.m. to 4:00 a.m. made it impossible to spend much. And by then I had received notice to report for duty in the Army on Nov 5, 1951 just a few weeks away. I was desperate to sell or get rid of the business so that I could go on a wild fling before my service call.

I spoke to my old friend Billy Vasiliou about taking it over and leasing it from me for $75.00 per week but Billy didn't want to leave Boston as he had found romance there.

Then I spoke to my father and he suggested that he had a cousin, John Lewis, who was about 50years old and was looking for a business opportunity. I signed over the business to my father for $1 and he gave it to his cousin under arrangements I did not take an interest in learning.

John Lewis lasted about six months in the business before he started to close earlier and earlier so that he could take the young ladies home and soon he was out of business.

I had become a "Summer Entrepreneur."

This "Summer Entrepreneur" made a net of about $8,000 that summer while waiting to go into the Army. It would be a long time before I would do that again.

During the next few weeks after leaving the business and before reporting for duty, I went on a spending frenzy in Boston to try and rid myself of the money I had accumulated. Every night with my friends at night clubs and bars I would pick up all the tabs but I was still not successful in spending it all.

When I reported for duty, I still had more than a little more than $2,000 cash in my pockets...

... and the Army started paying me $64 per month for serving!

SUNFLOWERS

As soon as my foot hit the sidewalk, when I was leaving our home at 82 Thames Street in Newport heading for school every morning, I glanced up to my right and the line of Sunflowers that my Dad had planted in the front row of the yard next door were all smiling directly at me. They were a well placed line along the chain link fence standing over 6 feet tall like soldiers in formation.

When I returned from school in the afternoon, this same line of Sunflowers greeted me with their big smiles even though now I was looking at them from my left side. The Sunflowers had followed the sun from East to West and they greeted me when I left and when I returned. It was almost literally the beginning of my day and the end of my day and even today that recollection reminds me of the biblical quotation from Ecclesiastes:

"One generation passeth away,
and another generation cometh:
But the earth abideth for ever.
The sun also ariseth."

So, as it was written, my Dad and my Mom passed on and my children came and I traveled to find the place where my family began so that I could prepare to understand the circle of my own life and see the rising sun. I searched the remnants of the Ottoman Empire where the Byzantine Greeks of our family had lived for generations from the days of Byzantium and Constantine to the days of the Turkish Republic and Ataturk. In the village of Kerassia, now named Kerasli, in the area of Eastern Thrace, were my roots but getting there was the story I will tell.

Traveling West from the city of Tekirdag in the early afternoon with our Turkish driver and my daughter January in the jeep in the summer of 1992, we turned at a left angle to head East toward the Sea of Marmara on a single lane country road better suited for travel by mule than by automobile. As we did this within a few miles, we found ourselves traversing the plains of Thrace.

I sat there with my eyes glued to the view in the fields around us, the stunning beauty of hectare after hectare of Sunflowers revealed to me for the first time why my Dad had planted that row of Sunflowers in Newport 25 years after he had last looked upon the Sunflowers of Thrace

The Sunflower Fields of Thrace

It was his way of remembering. That fourteen year old boy, who left his family and his homeland immediately after the devastation of the village in the major earthquake of 1912, was never to see either his homeland or any member of his immediate family ever again. Never again to feel the embrace and kiss of his mother Bourboi, never again to listen to the wisdom of his father Kyriakos, never again to hear the laughter of his sisters Fotini and Kyriakitsa, never again to tease his younger brother Haralambros, never again to have the protective arm of his older brother Gregory around his shoulders......but for a fleeting moment from time to time, he was back in their midst as he bounded out the front door of 82 Thames and caught a glimpse of those stately Sunflowers....it was his imaginary gateway to the plains of Thrace and his chance to be "Home Again."

When I was fourteen during the summer of 1944, I looked at the Sunflowers of 82 Thames Street for the last time as the next summer Dad would be moving our family into the first and only home he ever owned. He had accomplished great things in his journey of life and did not replant the Sunflowers at 118 Bliss Road because he was finally "Home" and there was no further need to look back.

When I write of him, I remember again how we lived and how mostly happy and sometimes sad we were and how loving and how much I miss them all and now the tears are starting and I will close this remembrance and say a little prayer as I glance at the Sunflowers standing outside my study.

Thanks, Dad

"I was thinking.....Vignettes of a Life Well Spent"

TA MARMARA

It took me 60 years to understand my mother's word choice.

I was 65 years old in 1995 when I made my third trip to the land of my origins....Eastern Thrace in Turkey. It was here on the banks of the Sea of Marmara where my parents were born in the little village of Kerassia, a locale populated by about 100 families or 500 persons.

Kerassia survived because of it's agricultural environs which gave forth fruits like grapes and cherries, after which the town was named since kerassia means cherries in Greek, as well as sunflowers from which the sunflower oil flows.

In addition, there was a significant industry making bricks on the shore of the Sea of Marmara. My paternal grandfather, Kyriakos, was a baker of bricks as was his father and grandfather before him that caused the family to be named "Psiroukis", which was a term to describe the worker who tended to the furnaces.

The village was located about one kilometer above the edge of the sea in a direct line which allowed for a clear view of this beautiful sea from many points in the town.

As I looked down on the sea, I finally realized why that body of water was named as it was...."marmara" in Greek means marble and clearly this body of greenish-blue water streaked with waves of white looked very much like a slab of marble and could be called "marbleized".

My mother left this village when she was 4 years old and she surely remembered the view of the sea when she went with her family down to the sea to take a fruit barge to Constantinople from where they would sail as third class passengers to the Promised Land...America.

Twenty one years later, she moved with her husband and two young sons from Somerville, Mass., to Newport, R.I. to set up residence in an upstairs tenement near the waterfront.

I remember that time very well as I was the same age that my mother was when she left the side of the Sea of Marmara. Every day when the weather was pleasant, she would take my brother, John, and me to visit a little park on Narragansett bay just a few blocks from our home. The formal name of that location was "Battery Park" but the locals called it "Blue Rocks" because of the color of the large rocks near the shore as the waves crashed ashore. It was a beautiful little park with a grassy area and a few benches to sit upon and watch

the few bathers and swimmers enjoy the sparkling water.

I also remember that my mother called that spot "ta marmara", a Greek term that means "the marbles". She used to say to John and me in a happy mood: "let's go visit "ta marmara" in Greek and we had no idea why she used that term.

When I reflect back on that time and with the knowledge I now have after 60 years, I realize that she was remembering the Sea of Marmara in Turkey. When I go back there from time to time in Newport to visit "ta marmara" , I also see the same "Sea of Marmara" that my mother saw as a young woman in a strange land that reminded her of her original home.

I am redeemed!

215

"I was thinking.....Vignettes of a Life Well Spent"

TA ORPHANA (THE ORPHANS)

Sometimes it seems a cruel use of language but to these peasant people it was realistic...the Diomandes kids lost their Mother in 1918. Consequently they were called "Ta Orphana" which means "The Orphans" in Greek.

In the Western world, politically correct people would rush forward to explain that these children who now lived with their Father and their Grandmother were not technically Orphans....but these people of the earth did not know such nuances and they could not bother with such trivialities.

There is a story about these kids that pleases...it seems that their Grandmother, who soon afterward died of the same Flu epidemic that had killed their Mother, took the kids in the early winter of 1918 to the Boston Common to play in the fresh air. Mary was 10 years old, her sister Sophie was about 5 years old and Damon, the baby brother, was 3 years old. They laughed and played with each other while talking in Greek with their Grandmother, Smaragda. Another group of women who were nearby with babies heard the Greek chatter and came over to introduce themselves as Greek-American immigrants from Lesbos and they began to talk about their respective families. Smaragda introduced the children as "Ta Orphana".

In very short order Smaragda, the Diomandes Grandmother, learned that they were the Bartis family living in Watertown, Massachusetts, and that one of the young ladies was now reaching the age for marriage...her name was Irene Bartis. There were 3 sisters in the family who lived with their older brother, John Bartis. The other sisters were Metaxia and Caliope.
Seizing the moment, Smaragda offered Irene Bartis an opportunity to meet one of her 3 young sons all of whom were off fighting in the war in the American Army. When they came home, this small frail woman promised to introduce Irene to one of them. And it happened....her son, Kyriakos (his American name was Albert) was the first one to be released from the service and he was introduced to Irene Bartis and the rest is history...they married in 1920 and then came Damon and then came Smaragda and then came Mary and then came Carl and then came Phyllis and then came Patsy and...
...Thus came about the Albert Diomandes family.

"I was thinking.....Vignettes of a Life Well Spent"

THANKSGIVING

The advertisements, movies and magazine articles all showed it as the most family of holidays...Thanksgiving ! But for the Parkos family it was another day of work, albeit a whole lot different than other days of work.

Dad, would reply to my questions...we are in the restaurant business and some of our customers depend upon us every day of the year as the providers of their individual family dining table." I thought he was right about that so it did not bother me especially since that was the one time all year that this little working class restaurant would prepare a full course dinner with all the trimmings elegantly presented to the extent we could do such a thing.

The price was set low enough so that anyone could afford it and would just about cover the cost of food so the labor and overhead was a gift from our family to customers who had no other with whom to share Thanksgiving.

The menu was wonderful...Turkey rice soup and mixed nuts for starters with loads of warm Parker House rolls and butter and then that gorgeous looking Roast Turkey with mashed potatoes, cranberry sauce, squash, rice stuffing with organ meats blended in, plenty of beautiful dark brown natural gravy, relishes galore, and the final chapter...servings of hot mince meat pie with brandy sauce layered on top and a large cut of fresh pumpkin pie with whipped cream rising like a snow capped mountain on top of it. Coffee, juice, soft drinks in abundance....no alcoholic beverages since we had no license to serve them. And all this for about one hour's wages for each of our special guests that day.

In addition and especially important, we gave them the chatter and playfulness of family as they ate their repast with us at the Supreme Lunch. Dad was right...we had to treat them like family for they were exactly that on Thanksgiving day. He taught us humbleness and a sense of duty to care for others...as it was spelled out for us in the bible by the teaching of Jesus:

"Verily I say to you, Inasmuch as ye have done it to one of the least of these my brethren, ye have done it to me."

217

THE 1918 PLAGUE

For every human consequence, a remedy is provided in the culture and traditions of the people of Kerassia, Turkey. And so it came to pass that at age 12, Mary Diomandes, an "orphan" when she lost both her mother and her grandmother during the Influenza epidemic of 1918 in Boston, was to be raised by her Aunt Irene.

That epidemic killed 20 million people around the world during 1918 just as The Great War, which caused the death of 8 million, was ending. The two deaths in her immediate family were devastating to this little girl who only 6 years earlier on the eve of her departure for "America" had seen the crushing death of her baby brother from the destruction of their stucco and stone village home caused by the Earthquake of 1912 in Kerassia, Turkey.

Their new life began in Boston in the fall of 1912 and Mary was with her father, Stergios, her mother, Styliani, and her maternal grandmother, Smaragda, living on Tyler Street just off Stuart Street in Boston, an area well known as the first stopping place in the new world for many immigrants. Within a year, a new baby sister was born and she was named Sophia. Followed within a few years by a brother named after his grandfather, Damon Diomandes. In 1918 as these deaths traumatized the Stergios Diomandes family, the children were Mary, age 10, Sophia, age 5, and Damon, age 3, with a father but no mother.

By September 11, 1918, influenza had spread to Boston's civilian population.

218

The remedy prescribed by their forebears was simple. The closest married woman related to the father was obligated to nurture the children. Stergios had lost both his wife and his mother and those were the only two women he was directly related to but his brother, Kyriakos, married within a year or two and his new wife Irene, from nearby Watertown, moved in with the family at Tyler Street.

To Irene was to fall the responsibility for raising the children of Stergios Diomandes and his daughter, Mary Diomandes, was to drop out of school where she had just finished the fifth grade, to help with the household chores and learn to manage a household herself

Irene, now the surrogate mother for these three children, was from a family named Bartis and their origins were a fishing village named Plomarion on the island of Lesbos. She had been educated more so than most in the old country and she was to be a constant point of reference throughout Mary's life. Many years later when living in Newport, Rhode Island, with her own children, it was very common for Greeks descended from the island of Lesbos to presume that she was also from that island. She kept her home in the manner of the people of that island and she cooked her food in their style.

There were two nicknames for Mary Diomandes and they were.."to orphano"..which in Greek means the orphan; and " E Mitilineisa"...which means someone from the capital city of the island of Lesbos, Mytiline, commonly used to refer to all people from that island? Aunt Irene had left her mark very indelibly imprinted on the child.

Aunt Irene was her mother, her teacher and her advisor in all matters and even many years later when Mary had her own family it was fascinating to watch her prepare for a visit from Aunt Irene...it was like an inspection from the most supreme commander in the military.

Mary's engagement was arranged by Aunt Irene and that whole episode is another story called "The Engagement".

"I was thinking…..Vignettes of a Life Well Spent"

THE EARTH MOVED

To: My Children

It was a funny kind of night – the sheep and the goat were restless and this caused them to move more than usual in the dug out earthen cellar which served as their pen for the night while the family slept in their stone home above.

The warm body heat and smell that rose from the animals gave comfort and peace to Panagiota as she dozed off to sleep.

An easy sleeper, it was never a problem for her to drift off. On the next floor pad her brother, a tiny tot named Ioannis had been asleep for some time as he was still a frail child having been born very small just one year earlier when Panagiota's father made his journey to America to begin his pursuit of a better life for his family.

The earth moved….violently….that night for Panagiota. When she jumped up abruptly, a stone from the wall of the house fell on her head and knocked her down onto the crushed to death body of her baby brother. With blood flowing across her forehead she cried out to her mother and grandmother for help.

They came to rescue her and soon it was all over….

Life would never be the same again for the little 4 year old girl who would be unable to forget the tragedy of that July 27, 1912 OS (Julian Calendar) - August 9, 1912 NS (Gregorian Calendar) earthquake in Kerassia, Turkey for the rest of her life.

Written by Greg Parkos in 1984 on a scrap of paper tucked in a diary.

THE ENGAGEMENT

The arrangement was started in the Boston Common, the public park in the center of Boston where the Greek women were walking their babies in the mid-day sun. It was 1928 and the world was good for the Greek immigrants in America....and as a result of some casual talk, one lady said to another that she knew a young Greek man from Eastern Thrace named Theodore who was ready to be married and the response from yet another woman was that she knew of a young Greek woman named Mary also from Eastern Thrace who was now of an age to be eligible. That is how the matter of an engagement began. Each of these women went back to the families of their respective candidates and suggested to them that a discussion begin.

In the case of the young woman, contact was made with her father Stergios through the aunt in whose home this young woman was raised.

Stergios looked like a stern man but he was a man of strong character and very good humor...he was a favorite with friends and family and was especially kind and gentle with the children. His life had been hard...a young immigrant to America in 1910 who had to go back to the old country in 1912 to retrieve what was left of his family after a very destructive earthquake. His two year old son had been crushed to death when their stucco and stone home tumbled down in the middle of the night and his only other child, Mary, was seriously wounded in the head but survived. His wife and mother were shaken up but without injury. Having successfully brought this family to America in 1912, his daughter Sophie was born in 1913 on Tyler Street in Boston (now Chinatown) and Damon was born in 1915 at the same place. In 1918 just as things were getting better and they started to enjoy the benefits of America, both his mother and wife died within a month of each other as a result of the severe flu epidemic called the Black Plague. Mary was the oldest of the children at 10 years of age and she was taken out of school in the fifth grade to stay at home and care for the house and the children as well as her three Uncles who also lived with them.

221

When Stergios' younger brother, Kyriakos married Irene Bartis two years later in 1920 they all lived together on Tyler Street and Aunt Irene took over the responsibility of raising the young children and managing the household. Mary stayed at home to help her and be educated in the ways of managing a household from her Aunt Irene. The new family unit moved a few years later to a larger tenement in Watertown, Massachusetts, as Aunt Irene and Uncle Kyriakos started a family. Their own children soon came.

In the case of the young prospective groom, it was not necessary to seek out family since he was of age to make his own decisions so contact with made directly with him by the lady who had suggested him as a candidate for marriage to this young woman.

After some investigative inquiries, a meeting was set to take place, of course, at the young woman's residence. That is how the courtship of Mary Diomandes and Theodore Parkos began.

Since Theodore was a single young man of about 30 years of age living alone with no immediate family members in the country, he was to be accompanied to the rendezvous by his cousin, Nicola Stratis, and his wife, Pagio, the family with whom he was living in Somerville, Mass. The place of meeting was in Watertown, Mass., where Mary, now 20 years old, lived with her father, Stergios, and her two siblings, Sophie and Damon, aged 15 and 12 respectively, together with the family of her uncle, Kyriakos, his wife Irene and their children, called Margie  and Danny, who were younger than her siblings. The house was a multi-story tenement and they occupied the second floor unit...with several bedrooms, a kitchen, a combination living room and dining room, and a single bathroom. The guests were received in the living room by Aunt Irene, Uncle Kyriakos and the father, Stergios.

Mary and the children were to remain in the kitchen until summoned for presentation as that was the custom of the times and the people. It was Aunt Irene's role as the woman of the house to receive the guests and introduce them to the elder gentlemen of the home..her husband and especially her brother-in-law who was the older brother and the father of the young woman who was the subject of the meeting.

Mary was trembling in the kitchen waiting to be introduced to their guests...she realized that now she was "of age" and it was time for her to be presented for marriage. When the guests were seated on this Sunday afternoon, Mary entered the living room from the kitchen carrying a tray with 5 glasses of water and 5 little dishes with a spoonful of sweet preserve on each one together with the spoon. Aunt Irene stood by her side as she introduced Mary to the guests and offered each one the dish of preserves and the glass of water. As she faced each guest, Mary said "Se Parakalo" which meant "Please" and then she offered her father and uncle the same things. Aunt Irene as the hostess did not partake but stood by her charge until each guest had finished the repast and then saw to it that Mary received the dish and glass of each one on her tray and returned them to the kitchen where she remained.

It was time for serious discussion. Theodore told Stergios that he had come to America as a young boy, had served in the American army during the first world war, had been a regularly employed house painter since the war and he felt it was time to get married and begin a family.
Stergios knew Theodore's family in the old country as they were both from the same village and he had no doubt about the family character.

Next, Pagio speaking to Aunt Irene directly as was the appropriate custom, said that Theodore was a good man and ready for the responsibility of a family. Nicola nodded approval. They all liked the girl. She was comely and obviously well mannered and had been raised in the traditional manner by her family. She would make a good wife and serve her husband faithfully.

Then Aunt Irene told all that Mary was a loving person who put all the members of her family before herself and that she was a good housekeeper and cook and would make a devoted mother.

Stergios was uncomfortable giving up his first born child and felt lonely at the prospect but he knew that Mary needed to be bethrothed before too long as she was into womanhood. Theodore was a fellow countryman so his character was assured. He agreed to permit the marriage if the two young people wanted it.

Mary and the four younger children were in th kitchen listening through the door to hear what was being said in the living room. She was frightened and shaking all over from nervousness. She didn't want to get married, she didn't know these strange people, she didn't want to leave her family but she would be obedient and follow her father's guidance...besides which Theodore was handsome and had a cavalier manner that she really liked....just like those leading men in the movies.

Aunt Irene brought Mary back into the room where some light discussion continued and Stergios suggested that an arrangement for their marriage would meet with his approval if they liked each other as they became better acqainted. No one was fooled by that alternative, everyone knew when the young man asked and the father accepted in their culture...the matter was settled.

Theodore asked for permission to speak to Mary alone. The living room was full with the other adults and the kitchen was full with the children. That left no alternative but one of the bedrooms where they went for a private meeting with the door slightly ajar under the watchful eye of all the others.

When they were alone Theodore told Mary that he was a good man and that he would care for her and he would be proud to have her as his wife..but..he wanted her to know about a problem he had. His voice was clear and strong so Mary knew he had thought carefully about what he was saying. He said "Mary, I am a passionate man in my love of life, country, and people but I am also a stubborn man and I need to tell you about that."

224

Mary waited demurely to hear the rest but she was already becoming captivated by Theodore's manner of speech and charming style. "If we are having a discussion and I tell you that the white sheet on this bed is black" continued Theodore "I want you to agree with me so that we will live in harmony".

He went on to say "Later, in a more peaceful moment, I will recognize my error and correct my statement to you....in this way we will be happy together in marriage." Mary agreed, for by now the notion of being married to this dashing man was becoming a romantic sensation. She never even considered her own needs or personality traits.

The engagement of Theodore to Mary was done !

Almost 50 years later when she told this story Mary did add this comment about herself which had not been spoken in that room: "The first time we had a disagreement and Theodore made a statement that he felt was a fact and I felt was wrong, not only did I not agree but I told him that he was crazy and wrong."

It was Mary's way of saying "me too" in that private discussion in the bedroom on the day of their engagement and she had a cute little smile on her face as she said "but it certainly was smarter to wait until later to reveal everything - our life together was marvelous."

Mary and Theodore were married in January 1929 and stayed happily together until death did them part.

I was thinking…Vignettes of a Life Well Spent"

THE GREATEST DAY

Not much different than any Tuesday in August, I was out of school for the summer and working at the Supreme Lunch with my Dad. My shift would begin at 5 P.M. and go on until 2:00 A.M. when we would close and take the next hour or so to clean up the place. That kind of a shift of 10 to 11 hours was not unusual in the restaurants of Newport, Rhode Island. Dad would open the store in time to be ready to serve customers by 6:00 A.M. and he would depart when my shift began. This day was no different…except that….

As I came into the restaurant and put on my white outfit and apron to take my place behind the counter, I noticed that my Dad was on the sidewalk in front of the Supreme Lunch and in an animated conversation with the lady who ran the art shop just a few doors away on Broadway. His arms were circling above his head as he jumped up the step from the sidewalk to the front door and as he entered the store, I saw that he was crying and yelling and throwing his arms up and down….as he called out to me "Gregory, Gregory, it's over; it's over; the war is over! God Bless America!". He embraced everyone he encountered and while crying kept repeating "This is the greatest country in the world".

That day was August 14, 1945. The day the Japanese surrendered and World War II ended in victory for the United States and its Allies. I was 15 years old.

My Dad have lived through another Armistice in the trenches of Europe as the First World War ended while he was serving in combat with the 2nd Cavalry of the American Expeditionary Forces under General "Blackjack" Pershing. He knew the agony and pain of war and he always felt that every American in uniform was his personal comrade in arms.

What happened next I think about every year on this day.

My Dad went to the cash register, turned the key which locked it and then put the key in his pocket as he turned to me with these instructions:

"Gregory, no one pays for anything from now on today. Tell each customer that Teddy Parkos says 'God Bless America' when they try to pay. Stay open until all the food and drinks are gone and then just shut the store for the night."

The whole city seemed to pour into Washington Square, the main meeting point in our town, and by 8:00 or 9:00 P.M. everything in the Supreme Lunch that was consumable had been given out with my Dad's greeting of "God Bless America".

We closed the restaurant then and did a quick cleanup so that we could go to the town square ourselves to celebrate. Never before and never again did I ever see what I saw that night in Newport, Rhode Island. Everyone was crying, and singing, and laughing and hugging each other with joy and affection especially with any servicemen that came into sight.

I was born proud to be an American from the stories Dad related about his love of this country but what happened to me that day elevated my passion to a degree that made me an American zealot. Now it was time to await the return home of our survivors. Some would not make it. It was a big price to pay but as my Dad grabbed me in his arms that day and kissed me with that day old growth of beard while yelling out "Gregory! Gregory!....God Bless America"; I realized that he would have been prepared to pay that kind of a price himself and that he would have expected the same of his American children.

In my book, Dad was no sunshine patriot and no summer soldier. I pray that he thought the same of me.

I will always remember the Greatest Day and Dad's reactions.

I was thinking…Vignettes of a Life Well Spent"

THE SUN ALSO RISES – DEJA VU

I have never been to Madrid since my first trip there in August of 1956 without following in meticulous detail the ritual outlined by Ernest Hemingway in the final two pages of The Sun Also Rises.

Pretending to be the narrator in the story, Jake Barnes, with my Lady as Brett Ashley…..we go….

….down to the Palace Hotel…and went into the bar of the hotel for a cocktail. We sat on high stools at the bar while the barman shook the Martinis in a large nickeled shaker.

"It's funny what a wonderful gentility you get in the bar of a big hotel," I said. We touched the two glasses as they stood side by side on the bar. They were coldly beaded.

"We'll have two more Martinis."
"Should we have another Martini?"

The barman shook up two more Martinis and poured them out into fresh glasses.

And then….

We lunched upstairs at Botin's. It is one of the best restaurants in the world. We had roast young suckling pig and drank Rioja Alta. Brett did not eat much. She never ate much. I ate a big meal and drank three bottles of Rioja Alta.

...I said "...Let's have another bottle of Rioja Alta."

"Let's get two bottles," I said. The bottles came. I poured a little in my glass then a glass for Brett, then filled my glass. We touched glasses.

"Bung-o!" Brett said. I drank my glass and poured out another. Brett put her hand on my arm. "Don't get drunk, Jake." She said. "You don't have to."

"I'm not getting drunk." I said. "I'm just drinking a little wine. I like to drink wine."

"I'll finish this," I said.

Down-stairs we came out through the first-floor dining-room to the street. A waiter went for a taxi. It was hot and bright. Up the street was a little square with trees and grass where there were taxis parked. A taxi came up the street, the waiter hanging out at the side. I tipped him and told the driver  *where to drive, and got in beside Brett. The driver started up the street. I settled back. Brett moved close to me. We sat close against each other. I put my arm around her and she rested against me comfortably. It was very hot and bright, and the houses looked brightly white. We turned out onto the Gran Via.*

"Oh, Jake," Brett said, "we could have had such a damned good time together."

Ahead was a mounted policeman in khaki directing traffic. He raised his baton. The car slowed suddenly pressing Brett against me.

"Yes," I said. "Isn't it pretty to think so?"

I never ever was able to finish the five bottles of Rioja Alta although I tried very hard to do so. However, I did eat a bountiful amount of Suckling Pig each time at Botin's.

But I had better luck in life than Jake in that my own Lady and I did have...   "...a damned good time together."

229

THIRTEEN

Of the thirteen guys in the suite, only one was married and he was my Uncle Dan, whose wife, Florence, was with him that last day in Washington before they were to depart for the war in Burma. She had brought her husband a gift of Aviator Sunglasses which she had helped manufacture at the Polaroid defense factory in Waltham, Massachusetts, where she was working in the war effort. They were Greek-Americans who originally volunteered to serve as O.S.S. operatives behind the German lines in Greece. Because of too many political entanglements of the resistance forces there, they were to lead Kachin tribesmen behind the Japanese lines in Burma.

Although nervous, the guys kept up a funny banter all day until it was time for Florence to leave for the bus station to return home and await the return of her husband from the war. The last "wise-crack" she heard before leaving was from Ralph Stratis, who although one of the youngest of the group, had been a instructor with the 101st Airborne Division before joining the O.S.S. Uncle Dan had known Ralph since they were boys together in Somerville, Massachusetts, when Dan's sister Mary, my mother, had married a cousin of Ralph's father.

Aunt Florence still remembers some 65 years later the last thing she heard that day from the group when Ralph laughingly said "What a bad luck number thirteen is! You can be sure that there will not be thirteen of us to return home after the war."

Uncle Dan & Ralph

Within months after that day in 1943, Ralph was killed as he prepared to drop into Burma for his final mission in Burma. The other twelve survived the war and came home as living reminders of the prophecy Ralph Stratis had spoken on that last day in Washington. Uncle Dan returned, he still had the sunglasses attached to his belt.

I was thinking…Vignettes of a Life Well Spent"

TOMMY, THE BOY NEXT DOOR

Charlie Fogarty was a plumber and he lived next door to the new tenement we rented in 1936, with his family.

We never did get much of a chance to see Mr. Fogarty as he left early in the morning and returned in the evening with very little social contact with anyone in the neighborhood. Mrs. Fogarty was also not involved with anyone and generally was at home all day. Their daughter was a young lady in her late teens or early twenties who did live a rather social life but it was limited to the evening hours and it was normally in the company of sailors. In Newport dating servicemen was a social sin that resulted in the girl being ostracized from the local community. That did not seem to matter much to the Fogarty daughter who was pretty attractive but being six years of age; I was not sure what anything in that regard was about. I just was fascinated by the whispering from neighbors when she left home at about 9 PM to attend to her social predispositions.

Tommy was a totally different matter. His bedroom was in the rear of their house and the window in that room overlooked the play area that was behind our home which area we occupied during just about all daylight hours when we were not in school. And, during all those daylight hours Tommy sat in his bedroom with his head thrust through the open lower window bellowing and cursing everyone in the yard while we played. Whenever the kids got close enough to the window, then Tommy would spit on them.

When I asked our neighbors what was wrong with Tommy they answered me that he was a Mongoloid and was locked up in his bedroom because he was like a wild animal and could not be let loose in public. I never did see Tommy anywhere but in that window. For over seventy years now I have thought about Tommy from time and time and how ignorant our society was at that time. Tommy was an innocent victim and it was the rest of us who were uncivilized.
God forgive us and grant Tommy a peaceful place in Heaven.

231

TWO BUCK LESSON

Working at the Supreme Lunch during the summer of 1946, I was the counterman, my Uncle Dan was the cook, and Rose McGinn was the waitress. Our shift used to begin at 5 pm and we would get busy about 6 until 8 and then there would be a lull until about 11pm when the night crowd would come in. During the lull on one particular evening, my Uncle Dan taught me an invaluable "Two Buck Lesson."

Since my Dad owned the restaurant, I was not paid a salary for my work at it was considered a family duty to help out at the business. I did receive my regular allowance very typical for a 16 year old boy.

Considering that payroll concept to be dated, I convinced myself that a fairer compensation would require that I enhance my status a little bit by "borrowing" from the cash register a buck or two from time to time. These loans would not have to be repaid, of course, and the practice was known as "clipping" in the trade.

I had been working with my Uncle for about a year now ever since he returned from the jungles of Burma, where he had been a OSS guerrilla operative leading Kachin tribesmen behind the Japanese lines. He was a genuine war hero and I loved him dearly. He was like a big brother to me since my Mom, his sister, had raised him from the time he was 3 years old when they had been orphaned along with their sister, Sophie, who was 5 years old. He taught me many things that a young boy needs to learn when he is in his mid-teens.

The Supreme Lunch was a working class restaurant and all three of us working that shift would ring up in the cash register the customers payment and return their change. So, during that busy time from 6 to 8 pm, each of us: Uncle Dan, Rose, and me would go to the cash register very often to take care of a customer's payment.

This night there was a two dollar bill in the cash register so when nobody was looking in my direction I decided to "clip" that deuce as part of my new compensation package. I swept the bill from the drawer into my hand and then poked my hand in my pant pocket to deposit it. It was slick…and no one saw it. I was cocky with my success.

About an hour or two later, my Uncle Dan put his arm around my shoulder and whispered to me:

> *"Greg, there was a two dollar bill in the cash register and now it's gone. I am concerned that perhaps Rose is stealing money so you should keep an eye on her."*

It was much worse than being caught stealing. Rose McGinn was a very nice middle aged single mother of 3 children who used to live in the tenement below ours. She was honest and hard working and devoted to our family for having given her the job when her drunken husband abandoned her earlier.

I knew my Uncle Dan very well….he was a brilliant guy and a straight shooter. And, I knew that he never suspected Rose of taking that money. He just figured out what I had done when he saw the two dollar bill gone and wanted to teach me a lesson that I would not easily forget. To reprimand me would have been just another slap on the wrist and no big deal. But to show me the true error of my habit, he conceived the TWO BUCK LESSON.

He Knew! I Knew! No One Else Knew! I Stopped "Clipping"!

UNRELATED RELATIVES

Once upon a time, in the Greek village of Plomarion on the Island of Lesbos lived a family named Bartis. No one remembers why they were given the name but it is assumed that one of the predecessors of this clan was an expert at shooting gunpowder because that is the meaning of the name in the Greco-Turkish language of the people of this region. Plomarion was a quiet fishing village which also proudly had a reputation for making sweet olive oil and very potent Ouzo, the alcoholic drink that was called "Milk of the Lion" because, although clear, it would turn white when water was added and drinking it made you feel as strong as a Lion.

This village and island were part of the Ottoman Empire since early in the Fifteenth Century during its ascendancy. However as the Twentieth Century began the Ottoman Empire was in serious decline and was often referred to as "The Sick Man of Europe." It was 1912 and the winds of war were sweeping through the Balkans and turmoil was rampant throughout the region. The future was mighty cloudy – like the milk of a Lion.

It was against this background that the Patriarch of the Bartis clan, Canelo, and his wife, Panagiota (Mary), agreed to let their oldest son, Ioannis (John), travel to America. But, they explained to him that it was his duty to establish himself in this new country, and to make a life for his three sisters there with him. John's sisters were named: Calliope, Irene, and Metaxia. By 1915, John had accomplished all that his parents asked of him and even added his brother-in-law Gregory Vouros who had married Calliope. And now, their story begins in America.

When Irene became 22 years old in 1920, a marriage was arranged for her with a young Greek man from Eastern Thrace, in Turkey, who had recently served in the First World War with the American Army and now wanted to start a family. His name was Kyriakos Diomandes and he and his brothers had come to America after a serious earthquake destroyed their village, Kerassia, in 1912. Time went by and Metaxia also married a young Greek man from Smyrna, Turkey, Theologos Cotatgis, who had also come to America after the Balkan Wars began.

Wait….more details to come:

Let's go back to that young man from Thrace named Kyriakos Diomandes. When they came to America in 1912, the four brothers brought with them their mother who was a widow, and the oldest of the boys, Stergios Diomandes, also brought his wife and daughter, Panagiota (Mary), who was then 4 years old. A year later another girl, Sophia, was born, followed by a son named Damon in 1915. They lived well and prospered until fate dealt them a vicious blow near the end of 1918 when Stergios' wife and mother died within 30 days of each other from the Worldwide Spanish Flu Epidemic.

The household was left with 3 single brothers, the widower, and his 3 children. Mary, who was the oldest at 10 years of age, had to drop out of school to care for her younger siblings and take care of the home while the men worked. This hard life situation continued for two years until one of the brothers, Kyriakos, was betrothed to Irene Bartis.

It was understood by Irene that she would have to take responsibility for the brother's family so, after marriage, she moved in with the larger family. Mary, at age 12, now had a new head of household to respond to and she remained out of school to assist and learn from her new Aunt Irene. Soon, the family moved to Watertown, Massachusetts, where Aunt Irene now started her own family of children even while raising Mary and her siblings.

The process of assimilation into the Bartis family began. Day by day, week by week, month by month, year by year, for almost 10 years Mary became more and more a part of the Bartis family. The children of Calliope, the children of Irene, and the children of Metaxia were like half sisters and brothers and the universe of friends and relatives treated Mary and her siblings as if they were truly blood relatives of the Bartis clan, although there was in fact no relationship except that Mary's Uncle had married a Bartis, which made Irene's children her first cousins.

This technicality never changed anything. Mary treated the Bartis sisters and their brother, John, as "family" in her heart and soul. The years have passed…and we are still the Unrelated Relatives….Mary's family and the Bartis family….and loving each other regardless of the DNA.

"I was thinking…Vignettes of a Life Well Spent"

VENGEANCE

It has plagued me for many years and I still do not have my arms around how to express it.

Ever since I began reading the history of the original invasion of Turkey by the Greeks in 1918 I have wondered about their war strategy and why they were so severely defeated after a dramatic successful beginning. It is not a simple story as there were many ramifications to what happened and who was involved but one fact of life I sensed as a consequence is:

"Vengeance for the Vanquished is Vital!"
"Vengeance for the Victorious is Vacuous!"

What does that mean? It means that if you lose a campaign, you need to find a reason for Vengeance in order to inspire your forces to overturn the order of things. It is vital for the vanquished….without a reason for vengeance, they have no strong reason to turn around.

On the other hand, the Victorious have nothing whatsoever to gain by committing acts of vengeance….it serves no purpose except to incite opposition.

The Greeks committed acts of atrocity when they invaded Smyrna in 1918 against the Turks because of their instinctive hatred for the Ottomans who occupied Greece a hundred years earlier…

…so they were repaid in kind by the Turks when the Greeks overextended themselves and the Turks turned around and pushed the Greeks into the sea at Smyrna in 1922 with widespread acts of Vengeance.

If the Greeks had spared their vengeance in 1918, would the war have ended differently? Who knows.

VISITING WITH DAD

This dream came upon me as I slept in Pamplona, Spain on July 9th, 1999 and represented the only really deep remembrance I had with my father since I last saw him in the early fifties:

I was walking down the steps in the street to the courtyard of my home with a long ago lover. She was walking behind me and actually touching the rear of my body with the front of her body as we came down the steps. I was trying to shield her so my wife Nadine who was in the courtyard could not see as I was trying to figure out how to get rid of her...another friend came down to my left to greet my wife.

And then my Dad appeared and as he came into the courtyard I went quickly to him and he slumped into a divan crying and I fell on top of him, hugging him and holding him tightly as he sobbed.

He said he was afraid and that he was losing his strength...that it was very hard for him just to drive up from Newport by himself in the car...I held him tightly and we cried together as I told him that he was my inspiration and how I noticed how much I was like him in so many ways with my hair line receding, etc.

Then I told him that I loved him and looked closely at him. His face was dark with stubble of beard. When I saw a glimmer of a smile in his face just under a flat hat that he was wearing, I kidded him about having a 70-year-old son..."Can you believe it, Dad?"

He stroked my head which was in his lap as my wife and Leah, who had arrived, were talking to me about getting myself more comfortable as I was lying in an odd position across my father's legs with my head on his lap looking up at his face.

There were two young girls who were with Leah (not her children) and one of them was looking down at my father with a look on her face and making some comment about how old we were. I told my wife to take her away immediately...in fact, I told Leah also to remove them both as they bothered us.

Then I looked deeply into my Dad's face and he sobbed "I wanted so much to go back and look at my village one more time before I die but it doesn't look like I will." My comment was that the loss of physical strength was the most severe aspect of growing older and that I had seen his village...it had not changed...it was poor. I mentioned that my wife Nadine was with me in the village and despite her young years, she was a perfect soul mate for me...knowing me and doing things I like to do. I loved her for that and in my way I was like my father, as he always liked the "American lady".

And I told him I had been intending to get someone to help him but then...he slipped away...the dream faded!

"I was thinking...Vignettes of a Life Well Spent"

WHEN DANNY CAME MARCHING HOME

He placed in my hand the most beautifully crafted pistol and holster I had ever seen in movies or in any other representation. This gift to me of a Italian designed Beretta pistol in a rich black leather holster with 4 German decorations of World War II including the Iron Cross was from a saint of a man.....but I go too quickly into my story so I'll slow down a little and begin again.

It was the summer of 1945 and I was a 15 year old boy who was mesmerized by the exploits of the fighting forces defending us against the evil Axis of Germany, Japan and Italy when Danny came marching home victorious.

Almost 4 years earlier, the bombing of Pearl Harbor by the Japanese on early Sunday morning of December 7, 1941 jolted me out of the innocence of youth. Sitting alone for a matinee movie at The Opera House, I heard the announcement on the public address system that "Pearl Harbor has been bombed by the Japanese and all military personnel are ordered to return to their bases immediately." My home town, Newport, was a significant naval base of operations. there was a lot of hustle and sound as the sailors left the movies. My heart was pounding and I was frightened by the panic-like atmosphere so I ran the several blocks home where my father was sitting by the radio in the living room of our tenement listening to the news bulletins. "Baba, Baba, what is happening" I cried out loud. Not a very proper way to approach a boy's father in the Greek custom of our home but I couldn't help it and my father permitted this transgression and he held me tightly when he explained that our country was at war because the Japanese had executed a sneak attack on the American base in Hawaii at Pearl Harbor. I only half understood the story but I was comforted that my father was in control and his hug, which was perhaps the only one I can remember his giving me, assured me that he would protect us. I have never forgiven this Japanese act of "infamy". On that day my innocence was lost.

239

Within days, almost within hours, the young men of our family and of our community were volunteering to serve…my mother's brother rushed to get married quickly and then went off to war as an O.S.S. agent behind the enemy lines in Burma, my father's cousin left Harvard College to command PT boats in the South Pacific, and a very sweet young first cousin of my Mother's enlisted to serve more than three long years on the ground in combat almost continually hand to hand from North Africa to Italy to Western Europe..on and on and on. That very sweet young first cousin of my Mother's was Danny, who came marching home that summer of 1945.

As best I can remember Danny was about 19 years old when he went to war volunteering as a foot soldier and a medic. The role of a medic should fall to the Chaplain's Corps as it requires an absolute wedding of both spiritual and physical strength. The medic is with the first wave of soldiers into battle but he is not armed with a weapon and protected only by a white armband with a red cross printed on it. Not much protection in the heat of battle. Danny first landed in North Africa with the first U.S. troops to see combat and later participated in the invasion of Italy under General Mark Clark where he was wounded for the first time in Sicily and then again at the Anzio beachhead. Never content with doing less than the most he could, he was giving medical attention to wounded soldiers at Mount Casino during that living hell of a battle that was memorialized in history as one of the bloodiest and most daring of the war. Each time, Danny was wounded while going to the aid of comrades who had been critically hit during these assaults. Each time, the wound was treated, the medal was awarded and Danny was back into combat within a few weeks.

When the war in Italy was nearly over, Danny and his unit went to Western Europe to participate in the invasion and conquest of the enemy in France and Germany. He was wounded once again, received not only another cluster for his Purple Heart medal, was treated for his wound and returned to combat again. He was one of the first of our young heroes to return when the war ended.

The United States Bronze Star was awarded to Danny with the citation that he…

"Left the cover of a knocked-out tank and rushed 70 yards to reach three severely wounded soldiers, to whom he rendered skilled first aid treatment. Although enemy machine-gun fire directed at him from a distance of 150 yards barely missed his body, and shell fragmentations whipped by his conspicuous figure, Private First Class (now Corporal) Diomandes disdained taking cover while he carried each man 50 yards to a covered position. He then dashed 70 yards through the same savage fire to render first aid to a fourth painfully wounded soldier and carry him 50 yards to a sheltered shed from where he was later evacuated."

When I think of Danny now, I reflect on the biblical verse that says "For God so loved the world that he gave his only begotten son to save it." I have never known a kinder and gentler man in my whole life. His good will toward his fellow man was legendary in civilian life as well as during the war.

And Danny came home that summer, took off his uniform almost immediately, left the war behind and began another life. He courted the beautiful young daughter of a local diner owner, Sophia Borodemos, as diligently as he had sought to give relief to his wounded comrades during the war. He won her over and they made a dashing couple…she was beautiful and young and he was gentle and loving.

Then came the children and a new diner and I drifted away over the next two years and I left Newport behind but I was never to forget Danny or his character.

When I learned of his death, I returned to Newport to be in his company one last time. My heart was filled with sorrow as I looked upon his children and I wanted to give them back that gift I had received from their father in remembrance of him but I did not know them and they were too young to understand the significance. On the other hand I could not keep that significant remembrance which Danny had brought back from the battlefields because it rightfully belonged to his family. After the funeral, I placed that special pistol, case and medals in the hands of one of Danny's siblings and asked them to pass it on to Danny's children when the time came for them to understand.

I have no knowledge of what happened to that Pistol but Danny will always live on in my heart.

"I was thinking…Vignettes of a Life Well Spent"

WHEN TOMMY MET ESTELLE

The winds of war were in the air and military preparation was starting to increase in Newport while Europe was aflame with conflict as the summer of 1939 ended. The mood in America was gradually shifting toward an acceptance of the eventuality of participation in the hostilities but not just yet. The direction was clear to those who watched what was happening in Europe.

It was against this background that Teddy Parkos began his search for ideas to incorporate into his dreams of opening a restaurant some day soon so that he could leave his job as a night watchman at the City's maintenance depot at the end of Long Wharf. He did not want to miss this opportunity to become an independent businessman, his lifelong ambition.

And so, on a beautiful fall day in September of 1939, Teddy and Mary put their two boys, Gregory and John, and their almost 3 year old baby daughter, Estelle, into the old Ford sedan and started out to visit some distant relatives in Hartford, Connecticut, who had a restaurant he wanted to see.

The drive was long but Gregory was entertained by his Dad's stories about his home village in Turkey and how he was related to the people they were about to visit. Teddy's cousin in Hartford was named Efstratios Antonio whose Uncle on his mother's side, Assimis Athanasiou, had married Teddy's Aunt, Fotini Psiroukis, his father's sister. There really was no true relationship but in the tradition of his people, this qualified Efstratios as a cousin to Teddy since they shared an Uncle and Aunt by marriage.

Teddy emphasized to his son that Efstratios was a very successful businessman who had owned several different restaurants and now had a special new diner that he wanted to visit for ideas. And he told stories of having known him in their native village and how Efstratios had in fact come to America in 1910 together with Teddy's older brother, Gregory, after whom his son was named. The original Gregory was actually the one who brought his little brother, Teddy, to the new world for a life of opportunity.

All of a sudden, his Dad turned the automobile into a parking area and Gregory jumped up in the rear seat to look at what was happening. As the car settled on the dirt driveway, Gregory saw the sign "Elmwood Diner" and realized that they had arrived at their destination. Teddy leaped out of the automobile and bound up the front stairs to enter the diner and quickly embrace his Cousin, Efstratios, and his wife, Basiliki, both of whom were working behind the counter. It took Mary a little time to take care of unloading the children and to prepare them to go into the diner to meet their relatives. There was only a customer or two in the diner so the families were able to enjoy a short chat before it was decided that they should all meet at the Antonio home in a short while for a real visit and dinner.

Teddy took a little extra time to look around the diner and then slowly took his family on a ride around Hartford and headed for the Antonio home in that city. By the time they arrived, Efstratios and Basiliki were home and plans were underway to prepare dinner for all. As they entered the front door, Teddy took his two sons into the living room to join his cousin, Efstratios, while Mary took baby Estelle into the kitchen to see if she could help with the preparations.

Basiliki was cutting vegetables on the kitchen counter with her two sons, Thomas and Teddy, sitting at the kitchen table keeping their eyes focused clearly on the visitors as they entered. Mary embraced the young boys and said to Thomas, who was the older of the two boys at 7 years old, "Let me introduce you to Estelle."

And that is how Tommy met Estelle for the first time.

And they lived happily ever after...

"I was thinking...Vignettes of a Life Well Spent"

WHERE HAVE YOU GONE, JOE DI MAGGIO

Joe DiMaggio died yesterday...March 8, 1999. I met him once and the memory will not diminish so long as I dream of heroes and idols. He was one of the greatest of these.

The first time I saw the great DiMaggio was at Fenway ballpark in 1946 when my Uncle Dan took me to see a Boston Red Sox versus New York Yankees ball game on a Sunday afternoon. A whole busload of men and a few ladies went together from Newport that Sunday to spend the day in Boston culminating in the ballgame at Fenway.

My Uncle had just returned from the War the previous summer and I idolized him as my personal hero for his exploits in that war leading Kachin tribesmen behind the Japanese lines in Burma. Dan was a very gregarious and outgoing guy so he was the center of lots of attention on the 3 hour bus ride...I remember all the other guys kibitzing with him almost continuously and especially Pete Pascale, the barber who had his shop next to Dad's restaurant where Uncle Dan and I worked.

When the bus arrived in the Boston area, we went first to the Prince Spaghetti House in downtown Boston for a pasta meal served with heaps of laughter and light banter. I was in seventh heaven...imagine to be accepted as a man in the company of men. And after the meal...the ball game.

It was the first time I had seen a major league ballgame and Fenway was awesome. On the field for Boston was one of the very special ballplayers I had revered...Ted Williams. And then, on the other side, wearing that elegant pinstriped uniform...the famous Joe DiMaggio.

Funny thing, nothing happened in that game of any significance and yet everything that happened on that day would be significant to me…a memory of Uncle Dan, Ted Williams and Joe DiMaggio. Heroes, Trustworthy, Elegant, Sportsmen, Only the best. And each had served his country and comrades well their whole lives.

The last time I saw Joe DiMaggio was forty years later in Hawaii. He was participating in a Celebrity-Amateur golf tournament being sponsored by American Airlines and I was attending a Whittaker Corporation bankers meeting at the same resort.

I couldn't believe my eyes…all kinds of sports stars hanging around the place all the time. Yogi Berra and Johnny Bench joined our group for some of the drinking and laughter time around the pool and in the nightclub after dinner. It was funny watching them as they both were relatively short and stocky and both wore soft caps all the time whether indoors or out. Johnny Bench wanted to dance all night with one of the banker ladies from our meeting who was over 6 foot tall…and I think Johnny was about 5 foot 7 inches or so. But they had a great time together.

As the night unfolded, I noticed Joe DiMaggio standing near the bar and he looked absolutely elegant in his double-breasted pinstriped suit with that white-silver head of hair. What impressed me the most was the way he stood so straight and with an air of dignity about him that no one else in the whole place could even begin to approach.

As I passed him, I held out my hand to acknowledge my admiration and he grasped it in his two hands and looking straight into my eyes, he thanked me for saying hello. I choked. No more words could come out; I just smiled and put that memory into my treasure house of wonderful things I have encountered in life.

Where have you gone, Joe DiMaggio? I will miss you.

WHICH ONE ARE YOU?

Surnames were not formalized in Ottoman Empire until 1923. Preceding that event the tradition of the Byzantine Greeks in Turkey used for naming their children had been in place for centuries…the first born son was given the baptismal given name of his paternal grandfather and his second name was the name of his father.

And so it came to be that the four sons of my maternal Great Grandfather named Diomandes Stergios from the village of Kerrasia on the European coast of the Sea of Marmara in Turkey, began their journey to the new world in the first decade of the twentieth century.

The oldest of the brothers was Stergios Diomandes and his first son was born in 1915 in Boston and was named for his Grandfather.

His name was "Diomandes Diomandes."

The second of the brothers was Kyriakos Diomandes and his first son was born in 1922 in Boston and was named for his Grandfather.

His name was "Diomandes Diomandes."

The third of the brothers was Ioakim Diomandes and his first son was born in 1932 in Boston and was named for his Grandfather.

His name was "Diomandes Diomandes."

The fourth of the brothers, Jossif, had no children.

Almost without exception whenever one of these three First Cousins were introduced to anyone, the immediate response was "Which One Are You?"

Although technically these men were given their father's name as their second name and this would differentiate them, most introductions are made with only the first and last names so that did not help.

To conform to the English language of their new country, the three First Cousins were given the more American name of "Damon" and the nickname "Danny."

The family decided that they needed a more personalized reference to differentiate between them. Over the years the names were changed by custom within the family and their circle of friends.

So, they became…

Big Danny,

Middle Danny,

and

Little Danny.

WHY DO WE DENY OUR CHILDREN?

Maybe it was about 40 years ago in 1957, when I first heard this bit of wisdom from Phyllis Rosen Brown, who was my mentor's daughter, my bosses wife, and was later to become a distinguished Professor of Chemistry with a worldwide reputation as a premier scholar in chromotology. She quoted me a line of wisdom that predated our new found gender equality which went like this: "Why do we deny our children the things that made men of their fathers?"

I started work at the age of 10 as a shoe shine boy in Newport, Rhode Island, and by the age of 11, I had begun work in a dry cleaning and laundry plant beginning at $6.00 per week and within a few years I was making $14.00 per week working after school 5 days a week and a full shift on Saturday and during the summer, we worked a full 48 hour week. I was not alone; there must have been about a half dozen of us of the same age that had similar jobs in that factory. The owner did not abuse us nor did he cheat us and, as a matter of fact, he gave us a great gift in that he expected us to do real work for our wages…it was no picnic.

The factory was hot and the work was continuos as we brushed cuffs of pants, ran the laundry tubs, pressed clothes and moved carts of dirty clothes from station to station until each item was clean and sparkling for our customers. On Saturdays we cleaned out the giant dry cleaning machines of their accumulated dirt saturated with chemicals and filter media…dumping them out of the filter bags into wheelbarrows and hand trucking them to a nearby dump site. It was dirty work and it was hard but each day that passed made me more of a man and was as vital in preparing me for a successful life as my formal education out of textbooks. That was 55 years ago and those lessons are still with me. My parents did not deny me the things that made a man of my father.

Today is a different time. Now in 1997, the do-gooders in our society have made it illegal for young people to have this gift.

In the vernacular of our time, our parents are denying their children the things that made men and women of their fathers, mothers, grandmothers and grandfathers.

I write this today because just this past Sunday, my housekeeper stopped by my home to visit with her 13 year old son, Danny, a sweet and charming but quietly shy young man of Mexican and Salvadoran ethnic background. His mother said to me "Danny wants to know how you became so rich" in a manner that was not in the slightest offensive but motivated by the awe with which this young man viewed my surroundings. I like Danny very much and I want him to be a great success so I wanted to really talk to him about winning in the game of life. My response to Danny was "Our society has denied you the opportunity I had to learn how to work early in life but I want you to get a job as soon as you are legally allowed to do so and to do a good job without regard to what the job is or your wages....Keep your studies up to at least high C's and B's and when you finish High School go on to some additional formal education but always keep your eye upon the "job" as that will prepare you better for success.

Today as I was doing some casual work, I glanced at a recent copy of the Reader's Digest and read 4 short stories entitled "My First Job" which started out with the story of Ivan Seidenberg, the Chairman and CEO of NYNEX, who talked about his first job at age 16 as a janitor, and then continued on about Shania Twain, the country music star singer, who got her first real job at McDonald's when she was 14, and the third story was J. C. Watts, Jr, the Republican African-American Congressman from Oklahoma, who started work at age 12 as a busboy every day after school until 10 p.m. and on Saturdays from 2 p.m. until 11 p.m., and the final story was about Gordon M. Bethune. Chairman and CEO of Continental Airlines, who started work at age 15 in a crop dusting business in Mississippi.

Why do we deny our children the things that made Women and Men of their Mothers and Fathers?

Danny deserves better!

251

"I was thinking…Vignettes of a Life Well Spent"

WOMEN OF SAIGON

It was early morning in New Orleans on July 26th, 1996 and I strolled to the famous Café du Monde for the traditional coffee and beignets for which Jackson Square is so well known.

On the bench alongside the wall leading to the kitchen sat 3 young Vietnamese girls wearing white shirts, black bow ties, and the standard white cap used by the wait-people at the Café du Monde.

I had to clean my glasses to look again because in a blur, these girls turned into the "the bargirls of Saigon" that I had seen on newsreels some 25 years earlier during the Vietnam war dressed in their multi-colored tight dresses designed to entice the Americans into an evening of fun and pleasure.

Moments later, when I reflected on this strange twist of vision I realized that these very well could be the daughters of those "bargirls" since they seemed to be in their early twenties and many of them seemed to be multi-racial.

Strange things come to mind when you look at people and think about them and their life stories…it is good to look and to think!

And always challenging to contemplate the universe in which we live and die.

WORDS FROM PANAGIOTA

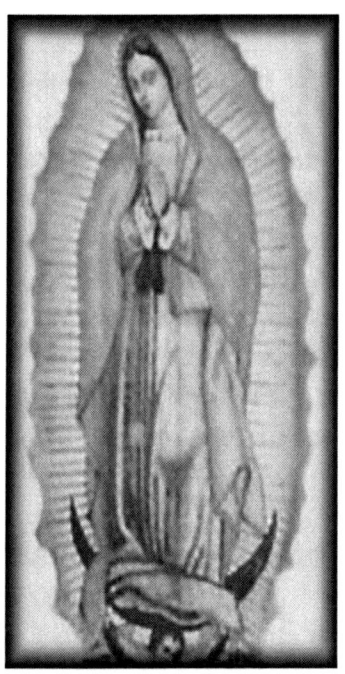

January M Parkos

October 3, 2000

Logic 7

Awakening Panagiota

I stood, staring into the eyes of the Son of God,
surrounded by music and golden light but my spirit fell,
more and more empty as my mind became aware, finally.
My father told me once, and I'll always remember, one
day as I complained of our weekly church visits, 'you must
go until you have learned enough to decide whether you
want to go'. My father always had a way of showing me
that he respected my intelligence and my will and
whereas some parents would say these things to appease
until words are forgotten, I knew my father to be true.

253

The day I turned away, the day my awareness became complete and my decision was made he did stand by me, he listened and learned through my eyes never trying to persuade as he knew I would do what was right for me.

The waters and oils baptized me as Panagiota, a tribute to my grandmother who I never knew, Mary. My Yaya died when I was a few weeks old but our connection is strong. She who foretold of my birth, she whose oldest son was the last to bring her his own oldest, she whose culture fused the deities of the church with the ancient Greek traditions and spirits of her peasant ways, it is to her image I have aspired. Always fascinated with my ancestral attachment to Greece, I began by looking at how the church had come to be so all pervasive in this culture, how the ancient deities were swallowed by this new religion. This of course led me to see the history of how Christianity adapted to each pagan place in order to increase consumerism and then turned against that which was so welcoming to difference in the first place. In this way, each exquisitely constructed stained glass window in the cathedral came to represent a conqueror of righteous tradition in my eyes. My sainted namesake became cold and unfeeling, a grand lie under her perfectly crafted face looking out from the front of the church.

The second step to my awakening was the thorough reading of the central text, the Bible. This document contained much hypocrisy. The book and the decisions the church made in its name went fundamentally against many of my own beliefs as well as many of the more general ideas presented in the text itself based on my interpretation.

I soon learned that this was also because the translators and biblical scholars took free reign over the book, sculpting it to reflect their mortal bias and social prejudices. Soon, the virgin, made a hallowed saint, became a young woman struggling with an unplanned pregnancy a new husband and a hostile world.

In a strange way I began to love her again, and aspire to this image in it's similarities to my own Yaya's struggle as a young girl coming to this country, lost in a world of words and traditions she did not understand.

I knew the art and beauty of the ritual of the church would always be with me, but now I had to find a means of accessing the ritual I so loved without the hypocrisies of the dogma of the church. Through a long process I finally came to embrace my own form of paganism. I never gave up on the values and traditions of my orthodox-orthodox upbringing but I embraced a more personal method of understanding the universe and myself.

Now, I look back and know all that happened was right, and I would not go back to pure acceptance without question. I still go to church; I can now finally accept the practice of Christianity as I always preached that they should accept my practice of paganism. Walking into any place of worship now, from Mosques in Egypt to Hindu temples in Chicago, to the Notre Dame I am overwhelmed not by the presence of any particular deity but by the power of devoted worship and true belief. I cannot deny any person the ability to believe, it is not a weakness but strength – I have come to accept faith even as I challenge my own.

WRITING SHANE'S PALANCA

"Whether it is clear to you or not, surely the universe is unfolding as it should." That quote from the poem "Desiderata" begins this message on the meaning of life to Shane Hopkins from his Godfather, Greg Parkos:

As Shane enjoys the sunrise of life in his 18th year, so too do I relish the sunset of life in my 73rd year and write the lessons of that lifetime.

I have danced the most joyful Fandango beguiled by a pretty Gypsy girl's flashing black eyes to the applause of many and sung the saddest Laments with a tragic Flamenco guitarist to the sobs of a mournful few.

The sweet sound of applause has filled my heart and the screech of catcalls has given me headaches. Both celebrated and reviled, I have laughed with the joy of achievement and despaired with disappointment and failure. I have been poor and in need as well as rich and charitable.

In other words, I have lived my life fully so that when someone speaks of me after my passing, I want it to sound like an epic tale and not a short story. Life is like a stage play, as Shakespeare wrote, and every one of us but players each to play our part and enter and depart as the scenes are played out to the end. The trophies of youth have rusted in unknown storage to be remembered only in fleeting moments. The cheers of the crowd are now only a faint sound.

What is it that remains? No! Not only remains but grows stronger and stronger with each passing decade…it is the honest unvarnished love of family and true friends. Not the "Sunshine Soldiers" who follow you while you achieve more and more splendid things, nor the "Summer Patriot" who basks in the ring of glory that surrounds your championship exploits. True friends will be those very, very few people who will sit quietly with you in those times when you are hurting not looking for anything for themselves but rather willing to give of themselves to you. Put things in perspective, excitement will fade but the true love of friends and family endures not only for a lifetime but for eternity.